HUMOR'S HIDDEN POWER

Weapon, Shield & Psychological Salve

NICHOLE FORCE, M.A.

BRAEDEN PRESS ❋ LOS ANGELES

Cover photo by Abdulhamid Al Fadhly

To Mom
The wittiest woman I've ever known.

CONTENTS

The arrival of a good clown into a village does more for its health than 20 asses laden with drugs.

~Thomas Sydenham
(Seventeenth-century British physician)

INTRODUCTION

Serious things cannot be understood without laughable things,
nor opposites at all without opposites.

~Plato

It is often said that "laughter is the best medicine," but this aphorism fails to fully express the power inherent in humor. Although many books have been written about the benefits of humor and the positive physiological and psychological effects of laughter, *Humor's Hidden Power* goes a step further and reveals how humor has empowered people to overcome overwhelming circumstances throughout history, how laughter changes brain chemistry and functioning, how the genders use humor differently, and the ways in which comedians have used humor to heal themselves and others through the ages (from court jesters to Stephen Colbert). It consolidates and clarifies much of what has already been written, reveals what has not yet been reported in the fields of neuroscience and humor studies, and provides recommendations for the targeted use of humor to combat the most common sources of suffering.

Chapters one through six provide a review of the research and demonstrate the therapeutic and transformational power of humor. Chapters seven through sixteen offer recommendations for ways in which specific sources of humor can be used to cope with and overcome the ten most common causes of mental and physical distress: depression, anxiety, heartbreak, work-related stress, illness, financial loss, low self-esteem, anger, aging and death.

Suffering is not a funny subject, but *Humor's Hidden Power* reveals how approaches utilizing humor may ease and potentially end much misery.

1
HUMOR AS WEAPON, SHIELD AND PSYCHOLOGICAL SALVE

A person without a sense of humor is like a wagon without

springs -- jolted by every pebble on the road.

~Henry Ward Beecher

Despite the buffoonish imagery that comes to mind when one considers the joker, the clown or the pie-in-the-face comedian, humor is more than mere silliness. It is an advanced intellectual means of developing new perspectives and coping with extreme circumstances. A maltreated animal has two potential responses to an abusive master: attack to stop the abuse, or cower and flee to avoid it. He cannot disarm the bully with a witty remark or ironically imitate his master behind his back for his own amusement. One of the first government actions in Nazi Germany was the establishment of a law against treacherous attacks on the state and party that made anti-Nazi humor an act of treason, and there was a reason for this. Research has shown that humor is the most effective means of preventing the indoctrination of brainwashing.

Used as both a shield and a weapon, humor has the power to soothe the most wounded and threaten the most evil. These qualities speak to its inherent potential -- a potential that has not yet been entirely tapped or even recognized. Holocaust survivor Emil Fackenheim said, "We kept our morale through humor," and many other survivors of the Holocaust, POW camps, torture and abuse have shared his sentiment. The stories of these survivors and findings of modern medical research support the notion that humor is an extremely effective tool for managing our advanced awareness and for creating new perspectives to cope with otherwise unbearable environments or circumstances.

Humor has long been recognized as more than mere fun and games. It presents an alternative means of expressing criticism about injustices, arrogance, pretensions or hypocrisies that cannot socially (or legally) be expressed otherwise. Court jesters could say things to the royals "in jest" that others would have been beheaded for uttering. When King James I of England had trouble fattening up his horses, court jester Archibald Armstrong reportedly suggested that His Majesty make the horses bishops and they would fatten in no time.

Most people know that "schadenfreude," defined as satisfaction or pleasure experienced as a result of the misfortunes of others, is German in origin. But most aren't aware that "gallows humor" was also coined by the Germans. The original term, *Galgenhumor,* has been traced to the 1848 revolutions and refers to cynical humor that derives from stressful or traumatic situations. Antonin Obrdlik said that "gallows humor is an index of strength or morale on the part of oppressed peoples," and it has historically been associated with the persecuted and condemned. An example of gallows humor can be seen in the Soviet-era joke in which two Russians debate who is greater, Joseph Stalin or Herbert Hoover. "Hoover taught the Americans not to drink," says one. "Yes, but Stalin taught the Russians not to eat," replies the other. Placing a comical spin on dire circumstances that are outside one's control was an effective coping mechanism long before the Germans named the phenomenon, and continues to serve the oppressed, victimized and suffering today.

Gallows humor is often viewed as an expression of resilience and hope that has the power to soothe suffering, but when a minority has few tools to combat an oppressive majority, gallows humor can be used as a sort of secret, subversive weapon. The fear of the weapon of humor was alive and well in Nazi Germany, and it was dangerous business for those who attempted to use it. The legal code of the time reflected Goebbels' interpretation of the political joke as "a remnant of liberalism" that threatened the Nazi state. Not only was joke-telling made illegal, but those who told jokes were labeled "asocial" -- a segment of society frequently sent to concentration camps. Hitler's second-in-command, Hermann Goering, referred to anti-Nazi humor as "an act against the will of the Fuehrer ... and against the State and the Nazi Government," and the crime was punishable by death. Article III, section 2 of the 1941 code (the *Reichsgesetzblatt I*) stated:

> *In cases where it is not specifically provided for, the death penalty will be imposed whenever the crime reveals an unusually low mentality or is especially serious for other reasons; in such cases the death penalty may also be imposed against juvenile criminals.*

Since Nazi informants could be within earshot at any given moment, it was important to hold one's tongue and suppress any witty desires. A Nazi prosecutor revealed that he determined the severity of punishment for a joke based on the following theory: "The better the joke, the more dangerous its effect, therefore, the greater punishment." Among those executed for Anti-Nazi humor was a Catholic priest named Josef Müller. Müller received a death sentence for sharing the following joke with two of his parishioners:

> *A fatally wounded German soldier asked his chaplain to grant one final wish. "Place a picture of Hitler on one side of me, and a picture of Goering on the other side. That way I can die like Jesus, between two thieves."*

This joke was said to be "A betrayal of the people, the Führer and the Reich."

In 1943, SS Commander Heinrich Himmler went even further in the fight against comical assaults on the Nazi authority when he issued an order making it a criminal act to name domesticated animals "Adolf." Whereas all citizens living under Nazi rule were subject to these anti-humor laws, Jews were more likely to be sentenced to death while non-Jews typically received only brief prison terms or fines.

6

In *Night,* a memoir written by Elie Wiesel about his time in Auschwitz and Buchenwald, the author discussed humor in the concentration camps and the macabre forms it took:

> *In Treblinka, where a day's food was some stale bread and a cup of rotting soup, one prisoner cautions a fellow inmate against gluttony. "Hey Moshe, don't overeat. Think of us who will have to carry you."*

The fact that humor persisted in and out of concentration camps during the Nazi era despite potentially severe repercussions demonstrates the vital role it plays in human resilience and survival. The inherently soothing and reassuring qualities that gallows humor confers seem to create a buffer of sorts between the sufferer and the source of the suffering. Without this buffer, the pain would be unremitting -- the sadistic intention of the Nazi regime. That is what made it worth risking everything for.

Concentration camp jokes reflected an acute awareness of the dire conditions and tragic fate that awaited its denizens. Since such an awareness would naturally produce a state of profound depression, the fact that it produced an opportunity for brief pleasure indicates that the jokes served to counteract the effects of depression. In much the same way that the release of white blood cells is the body's natural means of combating an intruding infection, gallows humor and humor in general could be the natural psychological means of combating an intruding depression.

A study published in the December 4, 2003 issue of *Neuron* reported that humor has similar effects on the brain as drug-induced euphoria. Using functional MRI (fMRI) scans, the researchers measured brain activity in 16 adults viewing funny versus non-funny cartoons. The brain scans indicated that humor not only stimulated the language processing centers of the brain, but also stimulated the reward centers, leading to the release of dopamine, a powerful neurotransmitter involved in the regulation of the pleasure-reward system.

Although laughter may seem impossible when one is immersed in the depths of depression, humor-informed therapies present a viable option for enhancing brain chemistry and regulating the pleasure-reward system. Such therapies can potentially recalibrate the pleasure-reward centers of the depressed and anxious, and greatly reduce suffering.

Theorist Martin Armstrong, who wrote about the function of laughter in society, may have described the powerfully positive effects of humor best when he wrote:

For a few moments, under the spell of laughter, the whole man is completely and gloriously alive: body, mind and soul vibrate in unison ... the mind flings open its doors and windows ... its foul and secret places are ventilated and sweetened.

2
HUMOR'S PHYSIOLOGICAL AND PSYCHOLOGICAL EFFECTS

Humor is mankind's greatest blessing.

~Mark Twain

Try to remember a funny story, joke or situation and allow yourself to smile and laugh out loud. Now laugh a little louder. Do you notice a change in how you feel? Do you feel a little more energized, a little more positive, a general sense of well-being? Laughter researchers Dr. Lee Berk and Dr. Stanley Tan of Loma Linda University in California have discovered that laughter not only lifts our spirits, but also improves our physical health by reducing stress, lowering our blood pressure, increasing our oxygen intake, boosting our immune system and reducing our risk of heart disease and strokes. It also causes the release of endorphins, our body's natural painkiller, and serotonin. Many popular antidepressants target the neurotransmitter serotonin by either blocking its reuptake or increasing production, but one can "self-medicate" using one's own serotonin supply by watching a funny movie, going to a comedy show, reading a humorous book or playing a fun game. For the rejected lover or laid off worker, this self-induced boost of serotonin activates a neurochemical reaction that enhances their ability to tolerate the stress response and think creatively of coping options. In this way, humor can be a highly effective means of dealing with overwhelming emotion and taking control of painful situations.

Dr. Hunter "Patch" Adams, the physician portrayed by Robin Williams in the eponymous movie, continues to use laughter as a primary tool in his treatment of terminally ill patients, to great success. He and several volunteers dress as clowns every year and travel to orphanages, hospitals and hospices around the world, bringing both joy and health to the residents. He is just one example of many who have witnessed and shared first-hand accounts of humor's powerful effect on both physical and emotional health. Eating high quality foods and exercising are essential to improving and maintaining our health, but a positive outlook and a willingness to laugh at oneself and the world can have significant effects, as well.

There are three generally accepted theories for why we laugh in the first place: the superiority theory, the relief theory and the incongruity theory. The superiority theory posits that laughter results when we feel superior -- in a higher, detached position from an uncomfortable or unfortunate situation. This would explain why we laugh at pratfalls and the misfortunes of others. The relief theory holds that laughter is the result of the release of tension -- it acts as a release valve for tension that would otherwise build and induce anxiety. This explains nervous laughter and laughter that results from very awkward or embarrassing situations. The incongruity theory says that laughter is the result of perceived incongruity -- we laugh because what happens contradicts our expectation of what should have happened. This theory explains why surprising things are often humorous. Someone jumping out of a birthday cake or a child playing with a jack-in-the-box come to mind. These theories are not mutually exclusive, and humor and laughter involve aspects of all three.

Regardless of which theory is at play, laughter has been found to induce the production of disease fighting cells called gamma-interferon t-cells and improve immune system functioning by reducing the production of hormones associated with stress. Existing drugs on the market that increase immune system functioning and encourage production of disease fighting cells frequently have adverse side effects that must be endured and monitored, but there are no negative side effects of laughter. It is one of Nature's greatest gifts to us, and to maximize its benefits we need to become more aware of how it works and how to strategically use it to combat what ails us.

When used as an adjunct to conventional treatments -- rather than as a replacement -- humor and laughter can be a significant disease-fighting tool that can help reduce pain and enhance healing. A study published in the *Journal of Holistic Nursing* found that telling patients one-liners before administering painful treatments reduced the patients' perception of pain. Those who were not told one-liners before their treatments reported significantly more painful experiences.

11

For those who are not ill but are merely inactive and unable to be more active, laughter offers many benefits as well. The process of laughing has been referred to as "internal jogging" because of the repeated muscle contractions and increased oxygen intake it induces. Repeated laughter can be a good source of cardiac conditioning. It can be particularly beneficial for those suffering from respiratory ailments such as emphysema since it cleanses the lungs by emptying them of more air than they can take in. Therapeutic deep breathing techniques work in the same way.

When we laugh we repeatedly take in large amounts of oxygen, an essential element of intracellular energy. Numerous studies have found that cancer cells are destroyed in the presence of oxygen, and it has long been known that many bacteria and parasites cannot exist in higher concentrations of oxygen. These are just some of the reasons behind the proliferation of oxygen bars throughout the country in recent years. As evidence of the health benefits of oxygenation continues to build, so does the interest in maximizing those benefits. But a comedy show or funny movie can create effects similar to those received from hitting the local oxygen bar, with repeated laughter oxygenating your blood and organs while you obliviously enjoy yourself.

In addition to its positive physiological effects, numerous psychological benefits of humor have been discovered in recent years. Psychologists Herbert Lefcourt and Rod Martin found that people who have a strong sense of humor become less depressed and anxious when exposed to stressful events than those with a less developed sense of humor. Additionally, psychiatrist Joseph Richman of the Albert Einstein Medical Center in Bronx, New York found that senior citizens suffering from depression and suicidal ideation were significantly more likely to improve if they had a sense of humor.

Psychology professor Peter Derks conducted research in which he and his colleagues used an electroencephalogram (EEG) to measure the brain activity of 10 volunteers while they were exposed to humorous stimuli. Dr. Derks found that how quick we are to laugh at something is determined by how fast our brain attaches an abstract meaning to the incongruity that is being presented. This explains in part why different people laugh at different jokes. Differences in demographics, culture, intelligence, personal interests, mood, etc. influence what we each are most comfortable thinking and laughing about. Dr. Derks conducted further research to more specifically examine the influence of one's mood on the processing of humor. He discovered, contrary to his expectations, that mood has little effect on humor perception or appreciation. While the emotional response to humor was found to be generated in specific areas of the brain, Dr. Derks discovered that laughter is a result of complex processes involving many different brain regions. It is therefore possible for an individual with damage to one or more of those brain regions to maintain the ability to perceive humor despite having an inability to laugh. Although there is a clear and undeniable connection between humor and laughter, the fact that the two phenomena are active in separate parts of the brain continues to intrigue researchers in the field.

The benefits of laughter can be obtained even if nothing seems funny or laugh-worthy. Researchers have discovered that just pretending to laugh and going through the motions will initiate the process and induce the positive effects that result from genuine, whole-hearted laughing. Dr. Lee Berk (not to be confused with Dr. Peter Derks) and Dr. Stanley Tan of Loma Linda University discovered that laughter optimizes the hormones in the endocrine system, which causes levels of epinephrine and cortisol to decrease and results in stress reduction. They were also the first to demonstrate that repetitious "mirthful laughter," known as Laughercise ©, causes changes in the body that are similar to those one would experience with moderate physical exercise. Researchers recorded enhanced mood, decreases in stress hormones and enhanced immune activity in subjects who engaged in Laughercise©. Dr. Berk concluded, "We are finally starting to realize that our everyday behaviors and emotions are modulating our bodies in many ways."

Laughter clubs have grown in popularity in response to the findings of Dr. Berk, Dr. Tan and others. These clubs employ laughter coaches who teach clients how to most effectively use laughter to enhance health. They organize groups of people to laugh together in 20 minute increments. Clients report that the practice clears their mind and enhances their mood for the remainder of the day.

Various forms of humor therapy have become mainstream and are growing in popularity. In addition to Laughercise© and laughter clubs, there is "clown care" which employs clowns to perform in cancer wards, nursing homes and children's hospitals. There are seminars designed to teach healthcare professionals how to most effectively use humor with patients. There is also a film subscription service for hospitals called The Chuckle Channel that is produced by humor therapy specialist Hob Osterlund. Her comedic alter-ego, Nurse

Ivy Push, acts as the channel's host. Seventeenth-century British physician Thomas Sydenham said that "The arrival of a good clown into a village does more for its health than 20 asses laden with drugs," and these humorous health care practitioners are proving the truth of that observation every day.

3
THE SUBVERSIVE POWER OF HUMOR

Una risata vi seppellirà.

(It will be a laugh that buries you.)

~Italian Phrase

In the oldest known work of dramatic theory, the *Poetics,* Greek philosopher Aristotle wrote that an ugliness that does not disgust is fundamental to humor. The Arabic translation of *Poetics* identified humor with Arabic poetic themes such as the satirical poetry known as hija. The focus of Islamic philosophers was more on comedy as an "art of reprehension" rather than the classical Greek focus on vicissitudes, comical events and happy endings. Translations of Aristotle's work in Latin and other languages further expanded and enhanced the interpretation and application of humor. In all languages and all theories, the common thread has been the power of humor to influence people and alter perceptions.

When he rose to power in 1799, Napoleon Bonaparte had serious concerns about comedic references to his personage. He immediately ordered the closure of all satirical papers in Paris and let it be known that cartoonists who toyed with his image would be dealt with severely. His most prized artistic representation of himself was Jacques-Louis David's *Le Sacre de Josephine,* which depicted Napoleon at his 1804 coronation in Notre Dame.

Two years before Jacques-Louis David painted *Le Sacre de Josephine,* English caricaturist James Gillray created a satirical version of the event that he called *The Grand Coronation Procession of Napoleone the 1st Emperor of France.* Whereas David's version depicted an exalted and elegant ceremony with a heroic Napoleon presiding over grateful minions, a noble Pope Pius VII officiating and a glowingly beautiful Josephine, Gillray's drawing showed the opposite scenario: a pompous, puffed-up Napoleon amidst shackled soldiers and slaves, a devilish Pope Pius VII and a bloated and acne-ridden Josephine. The finishing touch in Gillray's version was an image of Paris Police Chief Joseph Fouché clutching a blood-soaked sword with the caption "Bearing the Sword of Justice."

Upon seeing Gillray's drawing, Napoleon ordered Police Chief Fouché to imprison, without benefit of trial, anyone caught trying to smuggle copies of it into France. He also vowed that if he ever invaded England, he would personally go looking for Gillray. Even before James Gillray pushed his buttons, Napoleon demonstrated a significant concern about possible comedic representations of his image. In 1802, he tried to insert a clause into the Treaty of Amiens with England stipulating that any British cartoonists or caricaturists who used his image in their art should be treated in the manner of murderers and forgers. The English rejected the unusual amendment.

In 1830, a young French caricaturist named Charles Philipon, founder of satirical magazine, *La Caricature*, graphically depicted King Louis-Philippe's head in the shape of a pear. It was no mere coincidence that the French word for pear, *poiré*, also means "fathead," as Philipon believed the king to be both corrupt and incompetent. King Louis-Philippe responded by ordering production of the magazine to cease and buying all unsold copies in Paris. But he didn't stop there. In 1831, Louis-Philippe ordered prosecutors to charge Philipon with having "caused offense to the person of the king," and the artist subsequently spent two years in prison for drawing His Majesty in a comedic, fruitlike fashion.

When the Danish newspaper *Jyllands-Posten Morgenavisen* published twelve cartoons portraying the Muslim prophet Muhammad in 2005, a worldwide controversy exploded, Danish flags and embassies were set on fire, riots broke out in Muslim communities and more than 100 people died in protests. Referred to as the most significant crisis in Danish international relations since World War II, the "cartoon controversy" was depicted as a clash between the civilizations of the West and the Islamic world.

The fact that something comical, a cartoon, could cause multi-national unrest and lead to multiple deaths is indicative of the power of humor at its core. Satire is familiar to all cultures, as is the understanding that in addition to its humorous aspect, it also contains qualities of aggression and ridicule. Muslim protestors who threatened the lives of the Danish cartoonists were responding in much the same way, and for many of the same reasons, as dictators in totalitarian societies who had artists imprisoned for depicting them in a comical manner.

Interestingly, the protests that ensued were directed not only at Denmark and *Jyllands-Posten*, but also included the burning of German and Norwegian flags and attacks on Christian churches. Offended Muslims expanded their interpretation of the cartoons' symbolism to include a wide range of Western-generated insults and indignities.

In 2008, Danish police arrested three men for conspiracy to murder Kurt Westergaard, the creator of what was commonly perceived to be the most offensive cartoon -- an image of Muhammad wearing a turban with a bomb in it. Although the primary complaint was that any depiction of the prophet Muhammad violated Islamic law, Muhammad has been portrayed in many images in the Islamic world. The vehement and violent reaction to the cartoons not only pitted religious freedoms against the freedom of speech, but convinced many in the rest of the world that the Muslim community lacked a sense of humor.

It is important to remember, however, that the rules regarding acceptable forms of humor vary from country to country and culture to culture. Religious satire is commonplace in Western society, dating at least back to Voltaire, but it is unfamiliar (or very well hidden) in Islamic societies. Whereas Westerners have become desensitized to such humor through repeated exposure, Muslims have not; and many of them could not comprehend what was funny about ridiculing the sacred. The resulting shock and anger should not have been a surprise given the significantly different cultural rules and expectations about humor.

In 2006, Iranian newspaper *Hamshahri* held a contest for the best Holocaust cartoon and the winning entry depicted a bulldozer with a Star of David constructing a wall in front of a mosque. A picture of the Auschwitz railway station adorned the wall. The intention of the contest was to demonstrate that Western societies also have sacred topics that are off-limits to humor; however, no riots or significant protests ensued.

Part of the desire to appear to have a sense of humor derives from an awareness of the association between a sense of humor and modernity. A sense of humor signifies social flexibility and freedom while a lack of a sense of humor is associated with rigidity and lack of intellectual freedom. A willingness to laugh at oneself is a sign of social evolution that, when not possessed, can be a source of social exclusion and ridicule.

4
GENDER DIFFERENCES

Laughter is the shortest distance between two people.

~Victor Borge

For all of its benefits and advantages, humor can also be a source of significant social discomfort. Being the butt of the joke can be a painful experience, and confusion about how to respond can be disorienting. Much of the confusion lies in power dynamics: one's position in the social hierarchy determines to a large degree what is considered an appropriate reaction to this kind of humor. Those with less power than the joker typically respond by laughing along or by ignoring it. Those of equal status to the joker will joke back or challenge the comical comment as not humorous. Those individuals of higher status are more likely than the rest to respond by joking back.

There are also documented differences in the ways the genders use and respond to humor. Have you ever wondered why class clowns are virtually always male? Research conducted by professor of psychology Robert R. Provine at the University of Maryland in 1996 found that women who posted personal ads sought a partner who could make them laugh twice as frequently as they offered to be the source of humor. Men, however, offered to be the provider of humor a third more than they sought it in a partner.

Psychologists Eric R. Bressler and Sigal Balshine found that men expressed no preference for funny women, but that women tended to choose funnier men as partners. Rod A. Martin of the University of Western Ontario elaborated on this discrepancy between the preferences of the sexes when he said, "Although both sexes say they want a sense of humor, in our research women interpreted this as 'someone who makes me laugh,' and men wanted 'someone who laughs at my jokes.'"

Martin, Bressler and Balshine conducted research in 2006 in which they asked subjects to choose between pairs of potential partners for a one-night stand, a date, a short-term relationship, a long-term relationship or friendship. In each pair, one partner was described as receptive to humor but not funny themselves, and the other partner was described as very funny, but not interested in the humorous remarks of others.

In all scenarios except friendship, men chose women who would laugh at their jokes while women selected men who would make them laugh. Evolutionary psychologists have theorized that a sense of humor is a sign of intellect and strong genes and that women, the more selective sex due to the burdens associated with pregnancy, are attracted to funny men because of the genetic benefit that could be bestowed upon potential offspring. Humor and creativity researcher Scott Barry Kaufman of New York University believes this process, known as sexual selection, explains why the use of humor is important in the initial stages of a relationship: "When you have little else to go on, a witty person who uses humor in a clever, original way is signaling quite a lot of information, including intelligence, creativity, and even aspects of their personality such as playfulness and openness to experience."

An interesting study that examined the desirability of funny men to ovulating women was conducted in 2006 by Geoffrey Miller of the University of New Mexico and Martie Haselton of the University of California, Los Angeles. The researchers had female subjects read descriptions of poor but creative men and wealthy but uncreative men and rate each man's desirability. Miller and Haselton found that during times of high fertility, women chose poor creative men twice as often as wealthy uncreative men for short-term relationships. No preference was found for long-term relationships, however. In addition to the attraction women feel toward funny men, men find women more attractive when they laugh. This could be due to the fact that laughter signifies enjoyment and interest, or connection and understanding -- all desirable qualities in a potential mate.

Psychology professor Robert R. Provine of the University of Maryland observed social interaction in various public urban spaces while studying spontaneous conversation in 1993, ultimately recording 1,200 "laugh episodes" (comments that elicit a laugh from the speaker and/or listener). In examining the episodes, he found that women laugh significantly more than men, and that both men and women laugh more at men than at women. Although men consistently garner the most laughs, research has repeatedly shown men and women to be equally funny when it comes to humor production. Ph.D. student Kim Edwards of the University of Western Ontario arrived at this conclusion following a 2009 study in which men and women were rated on the funniness of captions they created for single-frame cartoons. Edwards found that both men and women created an equal number of highly rated captions. These findings indicate that the greater laughter garnered by men is more a consequence of social factors than a sign of a superior capacity for humor production.

Women and men also score very similarly on tests of humor appreciation. Psychiatrist Allan Reiss of Stanford University scanned the brains of male and female subjects while they rated the funniness of 30 cartoons. Both genders rated the same number of cartoons as funny and ranked them in the same order of funniness.

Men and women are both funny, but in different ways that the opposite gender sometimes finds unfunny. While women tend to share humorous stories and take a narrative approach, men more commonly use one-liners and engage in slapstick. There are, of course, exceptions to this generalization. Comics such as Sarah Silverman and Woody Allen cross over the gender lines a great deal, as do many men and women in society at large. Research has consistently indicated, however, that these trends exist. While women tend to use puns, self-deprecating humor and wordplay, men are more inclined to use physical and active humor.

In 1991 psychologist Mary Crawford of the University of Connecticut conducted surveys involving both genders and found that men favored slapstick humor, hostile jokes and more active humor while women preferred self-deprecating humor and sharing funny stories. Similarly, when Northwestern University psychologist Jennifer Hay taped group conversations in 2000, she found that men were more likely to tease and try to one-up in their use of humor with other men. They were found to tease significantly less, however, when in the presence of women, according to research conducted by Martin Lampert of Holy Names University and Susan Ervin-Tripp of the University of California, Berkeley. After analyzing 59 conversations Lampert and Ervin-Tripp found that in mixed company women actually teased more than men, and directed their teasing toward the men. The women became less self-deprecating while the men laughed at themselves more -- a kind of reversal of the typical gender-specific humor tendencies. The researchers concluded that men lighten up on the teasing with women out of a concern that it might repel them, while women become more assertive around men to counter feelings of vulnerability and to gain more equal footing with them.

Chimpanzees being chased by other chimps can often be observed making laugh-like utterances. The "laughter" on the part of the chased chimp is speculated to serve as a signal to the chaser that it is an enjoyable activity that the chased would like to continue to engage in. The parallel to the human flirting experience is clear -- a woman who fails to laugh despite a man's repeated humorous attempts is sending him a signal as clear, and opposite, as that of the woman who laughs heartily at every witty attempt made.

Psychologists Karl Grammer and Irenaus Eibl-Eibesfeldt of the Ludwig Boltzmann Institute for Urban Ethology have demonstrated that laughter can be a very accurate source for determining the level of attraction between people. After studying mixed group conversations and the subjects' level-of-attractiveness ratings, the researchers found that the amount of female laughter accurately predicted the level of attraction between both partners. A woman who laughs at a man's jokes indicates an interest in him, and this indication of interest can spur even further interest on the part of the man.

As a relationship develops and humor becomes more about soothing each other and less about winning each other over, the typical gender roles in humor tend to reverse. Researchers have discovered that long-term relationships have a better chance of surviving if the woman is the one who is the primary producer of humor. Psychologists Catherine Cohan of Pennsylvania State University and Thomas Bradbury of the University of California, Los Angeles found that male humor can be harmful to relationships when they analyzed the marriages of 60 couples over an 18-month period. The use of humor by men during significant life stressors such as job loss or a death in the family was found to be associated with negative relationship outcomes. These couples experienced a greater incidence of divorce and separation than couples in which the woman reverted to humor under such circumstances. The researchers speculated that this may be a result of the more aggressive humor of males seeming inappropriate in stressful situations whereas the more soothing style of female humor serves to better bond partners during these times. It appears that male humor is better designed to win attention and affection, while female humor is better designed to maintain them.

Anthropologist Gil Greengross is known for his research into the role humor plays in flirtation and seduction. Of all the humor styles, self-deprecating humor was found to be perceived as the most attractive. Self-deprecating humor reduces tension and indicates a nonthreatening stance that puts others at ease. The opposite of self-deprecating humor, and therefore the most unattractive kind, is sarcasm or ridicule directed at others. Humor that comes at the expense of someone else's feelings divides rather than bonds; and although it might elicit a laugh or two, the research indicates those laughs will not be there for long.

Humor plays a role in relationships from the initial flirtation through long-term commitment, and knowing the differences in how men and women process and use humor serves one well in all situations involving the opposite gender.

5
THE WAY OF THE COMEDIAN

The secret source of humor itself is not joy but sorrow.

~Mark Twain

According to a tale in the Talmud, the prophet Elijah said that there will be reward in the next world for those who bring laughter to others in this one. A book about humor should, at the very least, devote a few of its pages to the Masters of the Art -- comedians. Although they typically garner less prestige and respect than other artists, they are no less creatively endowed.

All across the country, they are out there. As you read this, they are sleeping in their old cars or in dingy motel rooms, driving from town-to-town, enduring sleepless and uncomfortable nights away from home, arguing with difficult club owners, and boldly getting up on stages in front of drunk strangers who hurl everything from epithets to glassware at them. Why do they do this? To provide *us* with relief from our miseries; to lighten our loads; to share with us the joys and benefits of laughter. That is part of their motivation, but there is more.

People who choose to be comedians are, by their nature, highly sensitive to and exquisitely tuned into others. The profession requires not only the intelligence to think of amusing quips and interesting observations; it also demands an acute awareness of what impact those quips and observations will have on different audiences. They tweak their material or alter their delivery to create optimal emotional responses in wide and varying demographics. To accurately predict how different people will respond to a joke, one must first be able to put oneself in their shoes and perceive the world through their eyes. This sensitivity to the feelings of others also makes comedians especially sensitive to their pain. Relieving pain in others helps them to relieve pain in themselves. In this way, bringing us joy literally brings them joy.

Blessed with high intelligence and sensitivity, but often cursed with unpleasant or tragic circumstances, examples of famous comedians who have overcome traumatic childhoods or suffered through severe adversity abound. Both of Carol Burnett's parents were alcoholics and she grew up on welfare with her grandmother. Describing the first time she heard the audience laugh while she was performing, she wrote:

What was it exactly? A glow? A light? I was a helium balloon, floating above the stage. I was the audience, and the audience was me. I was happy. Happy. Bliss. I knew then that for the rest of my life, I would keep sticking out my chin to see if I could ever feel that good again.

Richard Pryor grew up in an Illinois brothel where his mother worked as a prostitute and his father as a pimp. Among many other horrors, he was raped by a teenaged neighbor when he was six and molested by a Catholic priest during catechism. After being expelled from school at 14, he became a janitor at a strip club and later worked as a shoe-shine, a meat packer, a truck driver and a pool hall attendant.

Humorist Art Buchwald's mother was committed to a mental institution when he was an infant and he was raised in seven different foster homes. Art expressed an awareness of the defensive value of humor when he said, "When you make the bullies laugh, they don't beat you up."

Comedic actor Russell Brand was raised by a single mother following his parents' divorce when he was a child. He was molested by a tutor when he was seven, was bulimic when he was 14 and left home and began taking drugs at 16.

Stephen Colbert lost his father, Dr. James Colbert, and two brothers when he was 10-years-old in the September 11, 1974 crash of Eastern Airlines Flight 212 near Charlotte, North Carolina. Following the loss, Colbert says he became withdrawn and more involved in fantasy role-playing games: "I was motivated to play Dungeons and Dragons. I mean, highly, highly motivated to play it."

In the biography *I'm Chevy Chase and You're Not*, by Rena Fruchter, comedian Chevy Chase detailed an abusive childhood in which he "lived in fear all the time." He recalled awakening in the middle of the night to someone slapping him repeatedly across the face for no discernable reason, and being locked in the bedroom closet for hours at a time as a form of punishment. "I was fraught with fear and low self-esteem," Chevy said.

Joan Rivers has admitted that she grew up a loner and that her unhappy childhood contributed to her success as a comedian. She said, "There wasn't one good comedian I've known who was ever in the 'in' group at school. That's why we look at things so differently."

Bill Cosby grew up in a housing project with an alcoholic father who was both abusive and neglectful. He, like many others who share his career choice, used comedy to create an alternative, happier world than the one in which he was living. Mr. Cosby said, "You can turn painful situations around through laughter. If you can find humor in anything, you can survive it."

To fully understand how comedians relieve their own pain when they bring laughter and joy to others one just needs to learn about what neuroscientists call "mirror neurons." We all like to think we have free will to act as we wish, but other people's actions have a significant influence on our thoughts and behaviors. Studies involving macaque monkeys led researchers to the discovery that just watching another person move will cause activity in the regions of your brain that would be activated if you were the one moving. This activation was found in neurons in the prefrontal cortex that were activated when a monkey watched another monkey reach for and break a nut. Researchers referred to these neurons as "mirror" neurons for their seemingly reflective qualities. If you watch a runner jogging down a street, the same area of your motor cortex that would become active if you were the one running will activate. If you observe that runner tripping over a curb and falling forward, your heart rate will increase and your own arm muscles will unconsciously flex as though you are the one trying to recover from the fall. In this way, the runner has affected you and altered certain aspects of your brain functioning.

The physical separation between people is bridged by a perceptual "oneness" created by mirror neurons. Comedians who induce laughter in an audience create a kind of positive feedback loop that transfers the pleasurable aspects of laughter back to them via the invisible bridge created by mirror neurons. Using the example of the runner tripping on the curb, imagine that you could control his body using just your mental will such that he was immediately up on his toes and running effortlessly again instead of in the process of crashing down to the sidewalk. If you intensely visualize actually getting the runner back up and on track, you will notice a physical jolt or lift within yourself. Those are your mirror neurons at work and that is a micro-example of what comedians experience when they draw laughs onstage.

The relief of pain and the amplification of joy are not the only purposes or ends of comedians. Their craft also fits well into Matthew Arnold's definition of art as a discipline offering criticism of life. Comedians induce us to critically examine injustices, hypocrisies and all that is pompous, overrated and morally questionable. While much of society spends its time laughing at the oddities of outsiders and those who are "different," comedians, as outsiders themselves, frequently direct their humor at the insiders: often those who have abused or been corrupted by their power. Comedians, therefore, serve a somewhat noble role in society by drawing the public's attention to those who have become arrogant or hypocritical, and discouraging us from engaging in behaviors that contribute to making one the butt of jokes.

John Dryden expressed this concept when he said, "The true end of satire is the amendment of vices."

In *Comedians*, the 1975 play by Trevor Griffiths, six would-be comics in Manchester, England take an evening stand-up course taught by elderly comedian Eddie Waters, a man with genuine integrity who used comedy to fight his way out of poverty and much suffering. Waters is determined to teach his students something more meaningful than just the technicalities of making people laugh, and his famous words cut to the heart of the art of the comedian:

> *A real comedian -- that's a daring man. He dares to see what his listeners shy away from, fear to express. And what he sees is a sort of truth, about people, about their situation, about what hurts or terrifies them, about what's hard, above all about what they want. A joke releases the tension, says the unsayable, any joke pretty well. But a true joke, a comedian's joke, has to do more than release tension, it has to liberate the will and the desire, it has to change the situation.*

Comedians and other comedic performers have entertained the world and kept humanity's vices in check throughout history. Eighteenth-century German scientist and satirist Georg C. Lichtenberg said "The more you know humor, the more you become demanding in fineness." Those who induce us to laugh contribute to the development of our better selves, and we should not underestimate their influence or importance.

As the most prolific creators and sources of humor, comedians are not afraid to talk about the fears and concerns that most people try hard to conceal or deny.

By not only bringing them into the open but also laughing at and minimizing them, the comedian puts himself and his audience in control and the concealed fears dissipate in the shared light of day.

We have all heard of the "Way of the Warrior" and the "Way of the Buddha," and we live the "Way of the Professional," the "Way of the Academic," the "Way of the Spouse," the "Way of the Parent," etc. But for those looking for an easier and more fun path to a happier, healthier life, the "Way of the Comedian" could be the way to go.

6

HUMOR, NEUROPLASTICITY AND THE POWER TO CHANGE YOUR MIND

A well-developed sense of humor is the pole that adds balance to your steps as you walk the tightrope of life.

~William Arthur Ward

A growing body of recent scientific evidence indicates that we have much more control over our minds, personalities and personal illnesses than was ever believed to exist before; and it is all occurring at the same time that a flood of other research is exposing the specific and many benefits of humor on brain functioning. The ability to change the structure and functioning of the brain through experiences, and the conscious use of directed thoughts to do so, is referred to as neuroplasticity. The latest research in the field indicates that the adult brain not only has the ability to repair damaged regions, but to grow new neurons; and that willful activity has the power to shape the brain in new directions far into adulthood. We hear a lot about the effects of illness and old age on the mind, but in the not-too-distant future, we will begin hearing more about the effects of the *mind* on the mind, and the power of the mind to direct and master its own fate.

One of the most thorough and accessible books regarding neuroplasticity is *The Mind and The Brain: Neuroplasticity and the Power of Mental Force,* by Jeffrey M. Schwartz, M.D. and Sharon Begley. The book examines the latest research findings indicating that the mind is not merely a creation of the brain and at the brain's mercy; it is also capable of acting as somewhat of a separate entity that can intentionally control and shape the brain (and thereby, itself).

The latest discoveries of how the brain responds to positive stimuli such as humor are opening doors to new therapies for depression, anxiety and other mental illnesses. By stimulating and enhancing the humor processing regions in the brains of the depressed or anxious, the chemistry of their conditions can potentially be reversed, or at least positively altered. Why not use the positive powers of the brain to counter its negative powers? It is a question that the fields of Positive Psychology and Gelotology are currently exploring. Gelotologists study the physiological and psychological effects of laughter, and practitioners of Positive Psychology seek to utilize personal strengths and positive emotions to build resiliency and psychological well-being in their clients. Both fields are sources of much research in the use of humor as a coping mechanism.

An obstacle to such therapies is the fact that researchers have repeatedly demonstrated that negative information has a greater impact on the brain than positive information. As a quick self-test of this concept, imagine that you won $500 in a raffle. How would that feel? Now imagine that, instead of winning $500, you lost $500 from your purse or wallet. Research indicates that the intensity of your response to each of these situations will differ significantly, with the distress of losing $500 far outweighing the pleasure of gaining $500. This outcome is so common that researchers have given it a name: the "negativity bias."

The negativity bias is a result of the fight-or-flight response that is activated during negative experiences but not positive ones. The adrenaline rush and increased heart rate that occur with the fight-or-flight response cause negative events to be experienced more intensely and imprinted on the brain more firmly. The challenge for humor-based therapies will be in how to apply the humorous stimuli in such a way that it has greater influence in shaping the brain than co-occurring, and usually overpowering, negative experiences.

The reason the brain gives preferential attention to negative experiences over positive ones is because of the potential danger and threat to survival that negative experiences represent. The brain's default tendency is to alert itself to potential threats in the environment, so awareness of positive aspects of the environment frequently takes deliberate effort. The most effective therapies therefore utilize research findings in neuroplasticity to develop methods of making the brains of clients more "joy-absorbent" than "fear-absorbent;" more responsive to the positive than the negative.

Of course, we all differ in the degree to which we respond to the negativity bias. Some people are perpetually cheerful and upbeat while others suffer from a complete lack of ability to experience pleasure or see the so-called bright side. Researchers have found that when the depressed look at photos of fearful faces, they experience greater activation in the amygdala (responsible for emotion control) than non-depressed extroverts. When shown smiling faces, however, the reverse effect occurs, and the brains of the extroverts respond with greater activity than those of the depressed. Tal Yarkoni of Washington University in St. Louis, a student of the human brain's responses to emotions, interpreted these results as follows:

Part of the reason extroverts seek social contact more often than neurotics may be that their reward system responds more positively to other people's smiles, causing the extrovert to feel greater pleasure when they are around other people. On the other hand, individuals high on neuroticism may have brains that overreact to negative emotions, leading them to experience more anxiety and depression.

Although some people have a natural predisposition to be more attuned to the positive, the fact remains that negative events have a greater impact on our brains than positive events. That impact often takes the form of even further vigilance regarding negative information and potential threats in the environment that must be constantly monitored. This vicious cycle is what leads so many people spiraling down rabbit holes of depression and extreme anxiety. There is a constant negative feedback loop at play that, if not interrupted or countered, can lead to significant psychological distress. Since negative experiences are frequently outside our control and unavoidable, one option we have to disrupt the negative feedback loop is to reframe or reinterpret these experiences. Finding ways to redefine negative situations in more positive or humorous terms counters the adverse psychological effects that would otherwise be experienced. While we have all seen the tragic news reports of fired employees who returned to their former workplaces to take vengeance upon those responsible for visiting such a disgrace upon them, there also exist many people who, upon being fired, viewed it as an opportunity to find more fulfilling work or discover a new talent.

People who are inclined to react angrily or violently can, through conscious awareness and the powers of neuroplasticity, use humor to redirect their thoughts and gain a more positive outlook. Those without a naturally strong tendency toward positive thinking and positive responses can develop these qualities by repeatedly mimicking the (often humorous) reactions of their more optimistic peers to negative events and circumstances. The negativity bias generally occurs outside conscious awareness, so the first step in countering it is to make oneself aware of its existence. The first time you complete a task, such as driving a car to a new location, you have to focus and fully concentrate on remembering which turns to take and what landmarks to look for. After you have taken that route several times, however, you are able to drive it with minimal conscious effort or awareness. You can let your mind wonder to other thoughts while you make those lefts and rights and pass the landmarks because the repetition has imprinted the route on the circuitry of your brain. The same effect is found when humor and other sources of positive information are used to counter the adverse effects of negative information. At first, the intentionally positive reactions may feel forced, unnatural and possibly somewhat difficult; but over time, they will become second nature -- a happier nature.

The remaining chapters provide specific humorous book and movie recommendations and famous humor-related quotes to help jumpstart this process as it pertains to the ten most common sources of mental and physical distress: depression, anxiety, heartbreak, work-related stress, illness, financial loss, low self-esteem, anger, aging and death. But you should not fire your psychotherapist or stop taking prescribed medication. Humor is one of Nature's most salubrious tools, but to maximize its effectiveness it should be used in conjunction with other recommended courses of treatment.

7
DEPRESSION

If I had no sense of humor, I would long ago have committed

suicide.

~Mohandas Gandhi

Do you know why everyone isn't in a mental hospital? Because there isn't enough room. Philosophers have long observed a dearth of happiness among humanity. Henry David Thoreau said, "Most men lead lives of quiet desperation and go to the grave with the song still in them." John Stuart Mill observed, "Unquestionably, it is possible to do without happiness; it is done involuntarily by nineteen-twentieths of mankind." And Abd ar-Rahman III, who reigned as the most powerful prince of Iberia for half a century, famously said:

> *I have now reigned about fifty years in victory or peace,*
> *beloved by my subjects, dreaded by my enemies and*

respected by my allies. Riches and honors, power and pleasure, have waited on my call, nor does any earthly blessing appear to have been wanting to my felicity. In this situation, I have diligently numbered the days of pure and genuine happiness which have fallen to my lot. They amounted to fourteen.

According to the most recent statistics, 25% of adults will suffer from major depression at some point in their life. The Centers for Disease Control (CDC) report that antidepressants are the most commonly prescribed drugs in the United States. Where the natural world has failed to provide for our happiness needs, we have turned to man-made chemical assistance. However, humor provides an alternative means of attaining happiness, or at least relief from our misery, for far less money and fewer side effects than antidepressants.

Depression, anxiety, post traumatic stress disorder, and many other mental illnesses are caused by neurochemical reactions within the brain. Whether the original source is a traumatic event, long-term poverty, job loss, the break-up of a relationship or any other external event(s), the illnesses themselves take form as a result of interactions that occur within and between different brain structures and neurotransmitters. It is therefore reasonable to expect that those illnesses can potentially be reversed using the sufferer's own self-induced neurochemical reactions. In other words, if that is the horse these disorders rode in on, then that is the horse they can ride out on. Using our knowledge of how humor affects us physiologically and psychologically, we can begin to alter our own chemical makeup and thereby combat some of the effects of depression, anxiety and other mental health ills.

Neuroscientist Elisabeth Perreau-Linck of the University of Montreal carried out a study in which she confirmed that we are capable of altering our own brain chemistry. Perreau-Linck had professional actors self-induce a state of happiness or sadness and used a PET scan to measure the serotonin synthesis capacity (SSC) of their brains. SSC is an indicator of how efficiently the brain makes the serotonin from its chemical precursor, tryptophan. The cortex and deeper brain regions showed significant differences in SSC activity for those actors who self-induced happiness and those who self-induced sadness. "We found that healthy individuals are capable of consciously and voluntarily modulating SSC by transiently altering their emotional state," said Perreau-Linck. "In essence, people have the capacity to affect the electrochemical dynamics of their brains by changing the nature of their mind process. This is a kind of 'positive emotion therapy' that anyone can use to modify chemical functioning of the brain."

Assuming you will have a 100-year life span, what percentage of that time do you want to spend laughing and happy and what percentage of the time do you want to spend sad or dwelling on life's more negative aspects? We all have a limited amount of time on the planet and only we, no one else, can control how we react to the adversity and struggles we encounter on our paths. There is an abundance of pain and suffering to be had and although some is unavoidable, we do not have to endlessly dwell on and exist in it. The power to overcome suffering and escape it is within all of us, but doing so requires conscious awareness and conscious effort. Those who wait for happiness and relief from depression rather than pursue it will have a long wait indeed. By picking up this book and reading this far you have demonstrated the requisite conscious awareness of the problem; now it is time to begin the conscious effort. Luckily, when it comes to humor, the "effort" is enjoyable and can often seem effort-free.

One of the most effective ways to reduce feelings of depression is to reduce sources of negative input -- avoid people, places and things that generate negative experiences. Many people feel mildly depressed after watching the violence and various horrors paraded across the nightly news. Instead of watching the news, watch something more positive. If your friends are people who constantly dwell on the negative and bring you down, try to turn your conversations and encounters to more upbeat topics and events. If they refuse, then keep an eye out for new, more optimistic friends. As demonstrated by the studies on mirror neurons referenced in Chapter 5, we are all constantly being affected by those around us in ways that are completely outside our conscious awareness. Making the intentional effort to create positive changes will alter all of the subsequent unconscious effects that people and your environment have upon you. This includes exposing yourself more to humor by watching funny movies and television programs, going to comedy shows and reading humorous books. Some depression-alleviating movie and book suggestions are listed below.

MOVIES FOR DEPRESSION (Synopses courtesy of RottenTomatoes.com)

Some Like It Hot (Tony Curtis, Jack Lemmon and Marilyn Monroe)

When two musicians witness a mob hit, they flee the state in an all female band disguised as women, but further complications set in.

The Jerk (Steve Martin, Bernadette Peters and Caitlin Adams)

> *Navin Johnson, an idiotic white man who has been raised by a poor black family, doesn't realize that he's white, until one day his mother finally tells him. Distraught by the bombshell, he ventures out on his own to start a new life.*

Monty Python and the Holy Grail (John Cleese, Terry Gilliam and Eric Idle)

> *This is an absurdist send-up of the legend of King Arthur and his knights' quest for the Holy Grail.*

Caddyshack (Bill Murray, Rodney Dangerfield and Ted Night)

> *An elite country club has to deal with a brash new member and a gopher intent on destroying their beloved golf course.*

Young Frankenstein (Gene Wilder, Marty Feldman and Peter Boyle)

In this spoof of Mary Shelley's gothic tale, the grandson of Victor Frankenstein, a neurosurgeon, has spent his life living down the legend of his grandfather, even changing the pronunciation of his name. When he discovers his grandfather's diary, he begins to feel differently, and returns to the family castle to satisfy his curiosity by replicating his ancestor's experiments. In the process, he creates one very unique monster.

Airplane! (Robert Hays, Julie Hagerty and Leslie Nielsen)

This is a spoof of the airport disaster movies. When the crew of an airplane is stricken by some form of virus, the fate of the passengers depends on an ex-war pilot who is the only one able to land the plane safely.

Monty Python's Meaning of Life (John Cleese, Graham Chapman and Terry Gilliam)

The Monty Python comedy team takes a look at life in all its stages in their own uniquely silly way.

Happy-Go-Lucky (Sally Hawkins, Alexis Zegerman and Eddie Marsan)

A Mike Leigh comedy, "Happy-Go-Lucky" is set in contemporary London and follows the adventures of Poppy (Sally Hawkins) a primary school teacher. A free spirit, she is open and generous - as funny and anarchic as she is focused and responsible.

Napoleon Dynamite (Jon Heder, Efren Ramirez and Jon Gries)

From the rural town of Preston, Idaho comes Napoleon Dynamite. With a red 'fro, his moon boots and illegal government ninja moves, he is a new kind of hero.

Fatal Instinct (Armand Assante, Sean Young and Sherilyn Fenn)

A spoof of the late 80s and early 90s suspense thrillers and murder mysteries, including Basic Instinct, Sleeping With The Enemy, Cape Fear and others. A cop/attorney (yes he's both) is seduced by a woman while his wife is having an affair with a mechanic

BOOKS FOR DEPRESSION

My Depression: A Picture Book, by Elizabeth Swados

When You Are Engulfed in Flames, by David Sedaris

Laughter Therapy: How to Laugh About Everything in Your Life That Isn't Really Funny, by Annette Goodheart, M.F.T., Ph.D.

If Life's a Bowl of Cherries, What Am I Doing in the Pits? By Irma Bombeck

The Hitchhiker's Guide to the Galaxy, by Douglas Adams

Naked, by David Sedaris

The Women's Daily Irony Supplement, by Judy Gruen

Duane's Depressed: A Novel, by Larry McMurtry

Driving on the Wrong Side of the Road: Humorous Views on Love, Lust & Lawn Care, by Diana Estill

How Can You NOT Laugh at a Time Like This?: Reclaim Your Health with Humor, Creativity, and Grit, by Carla Ulbrich

DEPRESSION-RELATED QUOTES

Sometimes your joy is the source of your smile, but sometimes your smile can be the source of your joy. ~Thich Nhat Hanh

Razors pain you; rivers are damp; acids stain you; and drugs cause cramp. Guns aren't lawful; nooses give; gas smells awful; you might as well live. ~Dorothy Parker

The world breaks everyone, and afterward many are strong in the broken places. ~Ernest Hemingway

I know God will not give me anything I can't handle. I just wish that He didn't trust me so much. ~Mother Teresa

It is better to light one small candle than to curse the darkness. ~Eleanor Roosevelt

Good humor is the health of the soul, sadness is its poison. ~Lord Chesterfield

You cannot prevent the birds of sadness from passing over your head, but you can prevent their making a nest in your hair. ~Chinese Proverb

There are as many nights as days, and the one is just as long as the other in the year's course. Even a happy life cannot be without a measure of darkness, and the word "happy" would lose its meaning if it were not balanced by sadness. ~Carl Jung

Live by this credo: have a little laugh at life and look around you for happiness instead of sadness. Laughter has always brought me out of unhappy situations. ~Red Skelton

Most folks are about as happy as they make up their minds to be. ~Abraham Lincoln.

8
ANXIETY AND FEAR

The mind is its own place, and in itself, can make heaven of hell and a hell of heaven.

~John Milton

Anxiety and fear occasionally visit all of our lives. When we give an important presentation at work, take a test, go on a first date, walk down a dark alley or travel to an unfamiliar place our minds and bodies naturally respond by going on high alert and attuning to the potential dangers and risks of these endeavors. A healthy amount of anxiety and fear prevents us from falling victim to those dangers and risks. Choosing not to go down that dark alley could be a life-saving decision. But an excessive amount can actually increase our risk of suffering negative consequences. The millions of people who suffer from social anxiety disorder, panic disorder, post-traumatic stress disorder and other anxiety disorders experience debilitating degrees of anxiety and fear that can significantly limit their functioning in daily life. The natural instincts designed to help protect them from the dangers they feared have become sources of fear themselves.

Humor can be a useful tool for both the mildly and excessively anxious to use to gain a new and more clear perspective on their worries. Humor has the power to transform the frightening into the funny through the reappraisal process. Not to be underestimated, conscious reappraisal of a situation has been found to have a direct impact on our brain and its functioning. Researchers at Columbia University and Stanford, including John Gabrieli, studied the concept of the power of reappraisal by having subjects look at a picture of a patient in a hospital bed and imagine themselves as the patient. They were instructed to imagine that they, as this patient, had been ill for a long time and had little chance of ever recovering. The researchers used functional MRI (fMRI) scans to measure the brain activity of the subjects while they mentally immersed themselves in the pain and misery of the patient, and found an increase in activity in the left amygdala region. The amygdala is responsible for the processing of negative emotions, but the left amygdala becomes particularly active when one visualizes fear-inducing stimuli. Gabrieli then instructed the subjects to image that the person in the photo was actually just more tired than ill and that they were well on their way to recovery. The fMRI scans now showed a decrease in activity in the amygdala of subjects and an increase in activity in the frontal cortex. The frontal cortex is responsible for higher mental functions such as planning and decision making. Gabrieli said, "What we're seeing here is the effect on the brain of reappraisal, and reappraisal is something we do every day whenever we are faced with an emotionally disturbing or stressful situation."

Reappraisal works in both directions and can make a situation worse or better depending on whether one focuses on the positive aspects or the negative. Gabrieli's collaborator, Kevin Ochsner, echoed this idea when he said, "This strategy of cognitive reappraisal is based on the idea that what makes us emotional is not the situation we are in, but the way we think about the situation."

Researchers have found that a person's ability to reappraise negative situations so that they have less of a negative impact is related to their attachment style. At one end of the spectrum are avoidant styles in which people are aloof and tend to be critical and uncomfortable in intimate relationships. At the other end of the spectrum are the anxious attachment styles in which people are constantly seeking closeness and become extremely uneasy when they perceive that others do not share their interest. The anxiously-attached experience more difficulty than the avoidantly-attached in suppressing or letting go of negative thoughts and reappraising negative situations.

Researchers have identified differences in the brains of people who fall into these categories. The avoidant types, it turns out, have significantly more activity in the prefrontal regions associated with reward and motivation when they encounter disturbing thoughts. The reward and motivation centers of the brain have been found to play a powerful role in suppressing negative thoughts. When an anxiously attached person encounters negative or disturbing thoughts, the active brain regions are those associated with stress and emotional processing. The stress and emotional processing areas of the brain are, essentially, the factories of anxiety. For these reasons, it is the anxiously-attached type of person who tends to have the most trouble reappraising the negative. Even so, researchers such as Ochsner and Gabrieli have found that we all have the capacity to build our reappraisal muscles with a little work. Marcus Aurelius recognized this truth long before the advent of the MRI when he said, "If you are distressed by anything external, the pain is not due to the thing itself, but to your estimate of it; and this you have the power to revoke at any time." Humor is an effective and enjoyable way of revoking that power, and is an option that should be seriously considered by all who are anxious and/or fearful.

Freud belied that laughter was a means of taking one's mind off common stressors, acting as a kind of release valve for the resulting fears and anxieties. It is no mere coincidence that the most common jokes are ones about the most common stressors: work, aging, death, relationship issues and sexual problems.

The following anxiety-alleviating sources of humor can begin to open your tension release valve and help quell the fear and worry within.

MOVIES FOR ANXIETY AND FEAR (Synopses courtesy of RottenTomatoes.com)

Love and Death (Woody Allen and Diane Keaton)

Woody Allen's Love and Death is a satire of all things Russian, from Leo Tolstoy and Fyodor Dostoyevsky novels to Sergei Eisenstein films.

Serial Mom (Kathleen Turner, Sam Waterston and Ricki Lake)

> *A sweet mother takes a little too much at heart for the defense of her family.*

There's Something About Mary (Ben Stiller, Cameron Diaz and Matt Dillon)

> *There's something about Mary that still bewitches Ted. Although he hasn't seen her in over a dozen years, since that shameful prom night, his heart still flutters at the recollection of her. At the insistence of his good friend Dom, he hires private eye Pat Healy to track her down in Miami.*

To Be or Not To Be (Mel Brooks, Anne Bancroft and Tim Matheson)

> *A bad Polish actor is just trying to make a living when what should intrude but World War II in the form of an invasion. His wife has the habit of entertaining young polish officers while he's on stage, which is also a source of depression to him.*

Waiting for Guffman (Deborah Theaker, Michael Hitchcock and Scott Williamson)

> *A mockumentary set in the fictional town of Blaine, Missouri in which creative citizens prepare a multi-media pageant celebrating the 150th anniversary of their city.*

The Birdcage (Robin Williams, Gene Hackman and Nathan Lane)

> *Armand and Albert have a home life many would envy. They share a long-term committed relationship encompassing their lives and careers and have together raised Armand's son Val. When Val announces his engagement to the daughter of an ultra-conservative U.S. Senator, what choice is there but to accept his decision with love.*

Planes, Trains and Automobiles (Steve Martin and John Candy)

> *A man must struggle to travel home for Thanksgiving, with an obnoxious slob of a shower ring salesman his only companion.*

Hairspray (Ricki Lake and Michael St. Gerard)

> *A 'pleasantly plump' teenager teaches 1962 Baltimore a thing or two about integration after landing a spot on a local TV dance show.*

Everything You Always Wanted to Know About Sex *But Were Afraid to Ask (Woody Allen, John Carradine and Lou Jacobi)

> *An in-name-only adaptation of the once notorious sexual reference guide by Dr. David Reuben contains seven episodes based on helpful questions answered in the book.*

A Fish Called Wanda (John Cleese, Jamie Lee Curtis and Kevin Kline)

> *In London, four very different people team up to commit armed robbery, then try to doublecross each other for the loot.*

BOOKS FOR ANXIETY AND FEAR

The Complete Neurotic: The Anxious Person's Guide to Life, by Charles A. Monagan

The Pleasure of My Company, by Steve Martin

Serious Laughter: Live a Happier, Healthier, More Productive Life, by Yvonne F. Conte and Anna Cerullo-Smith

Are You There, Vodka? It's Me, Chelsea, by Chelsea Handler

Bridget Jones's Diary, by Helen Fielding

Mr. Irresponsible's Bad Advice: How to Rip the Lid Off Your Id and Live Happily Ever After, by Bill Barol

Sheila Levine is Dead and Living in New York, by Gail Parent

The Education of Hyman Kaplan, by Leo Rosten

Decline and Fall, by Evelyn Waugh

Yellow Back Radio Broke-Down, by Ishmael Reed

ANXIETY- AND FEAR-RELATED QUOTES

Comedy is defiance. It's a snort of contempt in the face of fear and anxiety. And it's the laughter that allows hope to creep back on the inhale. ~Will Durst

Every faculty and virtue I possess can be used as an instrument with which to worry myself. ~Mark Rutherford

Do you want to know the surefire way to stay anxious? Don't do the thing that makes you nervous. ~Larina Kase

If you ask what is the single most important key to longevity, I would have to say it is avoiding worry, stress and tension. And if you didn't ask me, I'd still have to say it. ~George Burns

Anxiety does not empty tomorrow of its sorrows, but only empties today of its strength. ~Charles Spurgeon

The truth is that our finest moments are most likely to occur when we are feeling deeply uncomfortable, unhappy, or unfulfilled. For it is only in such moments, propelled by our discomfort, that we are likely to step out of our ruts and start searching for different ways or truer answers. ~M. Scott Peck

When I look back on all these worries, I remember the story of the old man who said on his deathbed that he had had a lot of trouble in his life, most of which had never happened. ~Winston Churchill

The reason why worry kills more people than work is that more people worry than work. ~Robert Frost

Nothing in the affairs of men is worthy of great anxiety. ~Plato

Good humor is a tonic for mind and body. It is the best antidote for anxiety and depression. It is a business asset. It attracts and keeps friends. It lightens human burdens. It is the direct route to serenity and contentment. ~Grenville Kleiser.

9

HEARTBREAK, REJECTION AND DIVORCE

The more I live, the more I think that humor is the saving

sense.

~Jacob August Riis

Social psychologist Daniel Gilbert of Harvard University said, "In many ways, navigating the social world is more complicated than a voyage to the moon. But it's a journey we have to take, because whether we like it or not, our happiness is in each other's hands." Our sadness is also in each other's hands, and is most easily induced by those we most love.

Rejection from a loved one can feel like the end of the world and can elicit profound feelings of worthlessness, loneliness and grief. Divorce can be a more painful experience than the actual death of a spouse because of the searing pain and suffering caused by rejection. It leaves one wondering why, exactly, they are no longer "good enough" for the other person's love, and questioning whether they are even deserving of love at all. Rejection causes us all to question our own value and can lead some to question the value of their very existence. We have all heard or read about the rejected lover who, in a fit of fury and despair, lashes out and kills the rejecter and/or themselves. The pain can be so profound and unrelenting that it strangles out all hope and literally destroys the rejected. University of Michigan psychology professor Ethan Kross and a team of researchers found that the regions of the brain that are activated when experiencing heartbreak are the same regions activated when experiencing physical pain. Like physical pain, this emotional pain cannot be ignored or escaped unless some form of anesthetic is applied. The natural anesthetic qualities of humor and its easy availability make it a good place to begin buffering oneself from the negative effects of rejection.

The suffering one endures from heartbreak should never be underestimated or minimized. It can be both debilitating and dangerous. It does not, however, have to be the end of the world. Rejection is a universal experience that we all, unfortunately, come to know at some point(s) in our lives. Movie stars, models, super athletes and other idols of perfection have been rejected, divorced and left behind by those they had loved dearly. With divorce rates currently pushing above 50% does that mean that 50% of the population is unworthy and unlovable? It does not. It simply reflects the fact that the human heart is mercurial and all of our feelings, including love, can and do change over time. As difficult as it is to believe, it really is less personal than it is just a consequence of being human. It is important to remember this in times of rejection because it is easy to fall into an abyss of sadness and self-loathing without a wider perspective. Philosopher Arthur Schopenhauer commented on the importance of taking this wider perspective when he said the following about a man who can achieve such objectivity:

> *In the course of his own life and its misfortunes, he will look less at his own individual lot than at the lot of mankind as a whole, and accordingly will conduct himself ... more as a knower than as a sufferer.*

Freud observed that all creativity derives from sublimation of the sex drive and the natural world appears to reflect this fact. Survival and procreation are Nature's priorities for us, and happiness and pleasure are the carrots Nature uses to direct our behavior toward the fulfillment of those priorities. The *hope* for happiness, not its actual attainment, is what drives us to create, achieve and evolve. If we attained perfect happiness and bliss, what more, then, would we strive for? What would motivate us to achieve and evolve any further than we already had? With nothing desired or desperately wanted, we would settle in our contentment and the creation process would slow or stop. Pain, unsatisfied desire and hope for something more play a significant role in driving human development, innovation, discovery and growth. Contentment and satisfaction, as pleasant and desirable as they are, are the destroyers of innovation.

To gain the proper perspective on heartbreak it is important to understand that Nature does not exist to serve us, we exist to serve the ends of Nature. Pain, unsatisfied desires and unrequited love are our natural motivators to evolutionary and personal greatness. It may seem cruel, but you will run faster if chased by a hungry lion than a fluffy bunny; and being chased by the lion will force you to develop survival skills you would never have to consider if chased by the bunny. As harsh as the inevitable pain and suffering imposed by Nature may seem, it really is for our own good. We become better, stronger people when faced with pain, including that of rejection, if we recognize it and use it for good rather than evil. Rejection is not without its rewards, which are growth, maturity and the potential development of a better, stronger self.

Although Nature gave us pain and longing to induce change and growth, it also gave us the ability to use humor to mitigate some of the more damaging and dangerous aspects of that pain. Suffering may be an inevitable part of life, but uninterrupted, unrelenting suffering does not have to be. Joy and happiness can be self-produced and self-induced by the rejected by partaking in some of the following laughter-inducing activities and endeavors. Learning to laugh at the relationship foibles of others can make our own more understandable and tolerable, and the following sources will do just that.

MOVIES FOR HEARTBREAK AND REJECTION

(Synopses courtesy of RottenTomatoes.com)

Forgetting Sarah Marshall (Jason Segal, Kristen Bell and Mila Kunis)

Devastated Peter takes a Hawaii vacation in order to deal with recent break-up with his TV star girlfriend, Sarah. Little does he know Sarah's traveling to the same resort as her ex ... and she's bringing along her new boyfriend.

Play It Again, Sam (Woody Allen, Tony Roberts and Diane Keaton)

Allan Felix is a writer for Film Quarterly who is consumed by movies, particularly his favorite film of all time, Casablanca. When Allan's wife Nancy leaves him and applies for a divorce, he is unable to deal with this emotional turmoil and seeks solace in the movies he loves.

Ruthless People (Danny DeVito and Bette Midler)

Midler is sublime as the victim of low-rent abductors ("I've been kidnapped by Kmart!"), and DeVito's the gleeful philanderer who refuses to pay ransom for his wife's unwanted return.

The War of the Roses (Michael Douglas and Kathleen Turner)

A married couple try everything to get each other to leave the house in a vicious divorce battle.

Definitely Maybe (Rachel Weisz, Elizabeth Banks and Ryan Reynolds)

> *A political consultant tries to explain his impending divorce and past relationships to his 11-year-old daughter.*

Get Him To The Greek (Jonah Hill, Russell Brand and Rose Byrne)

> *A record company intern (Hill) is hired to accompany out-of-control British rock star Aldous Snow (Brand) to a concert at L.A.'s Greek Theater.*

Under the Tuscan Sun (Diane Lane, Sandra Oh and Raoul Bova)

> *After a brutal divorce, Frances (Diane Lane) is persuaded by her friend Patti (Sandra Oh) to take a tour of Italy--where, on a whim that she hopes will rescue her from her desperate unhappiness, she buys a rundown villa and sets out to renovate it. Along the way, she gets advice from a former Fellini actress, meets a scrumptious Italian lover, and helps support Patti after her own relationship derails.*

Lars and the Real Girl (Ryan Gosling, Paul Schneider and Emily Mortimer)

> *Lars Lindstrom is a loveable introvert whose emotional baggage has kept him from fully embracing life. After*

years of what is almost solitude, he invites Bianca, a friend he met on the internet to visit him. He introduces Bianca to his brother Gus and his wife Karen and they are stunned. They don't know what to say to Lars or Bianca--because she is a life-size doll, not a real person and he is treating her as though she is alive.

Broken Flowers (Bill Murray, Julie Delpy and Sharon Stone)

The resolutely single Don has just been dumped by his latest lover, Sherry. Don yet again resigns himself to being alone and left to his own devices. Instead, he is compelled to reflect on his past when he receives by mail a mysterious pink letter.

Run Fat Boy Run (Simon Pegg, Thandie Newton and Hank Azaria)

"Run, Fatboy, Run" centers on a charming but oblivious overweight guy who leaves his fiancee on their wedding day only to discover years later that he really loves her. To win her back, he must finish a marathon while making her realize that her handsome, wealthy fiance is the wrong guy for her.

BOOKS FOR HEARTBREAK AND REJECTION

Things I've Learned From Women Who've Dumped Me, by Ben Karlin

A Marriage Made in heaven – or Too Tired for an Affair and I Lost Everything in the Post-Natal Depression, by Erma Bombeck

Western Swing, by Tim Sandlin

Le Divorce, by Bebe Neuwirth

Humor: Cases of Desperation Dating: How to be Successful at Making Fun of Dating, by Shirley Boykin

Southern Fried Divorce, by Judy Conner

Skinny Dip, by Carl Hiaasen

High Fidelity, by Nick Hornby

My Horizontal Life: A Collection of One-Night Stands, by Chelsea Handler

Sex and Sunsets, by Tim Sandlin

HEARTBREAK- AND REJECTION-RELATED QUOTES

Marriage is like putting your hand into a bag of snakes in the hope of pulling out an eel. ~Leonardo Di Vinci

I couldn't stand that my husband was being unfaithful. I am Raquel Welch -- understand? ~Raquel Welch

In youth, it was a way I had, to do my best to please. And change, with every passing lad to suit his theories. But now I know the things I know, and I do the things I do; and if you do not like me so, to hell, my love, with you. ~Dorothy Parker

Do you know what it means to come home at night to a woman who'll give you a little love, a little affection, a little tenderness? It means you're in the wrong house. ~Henny Youngman

Love is a snowmobile racing across the tundra and then suddenly it flips over, pinning you underneath. At night, the ice weasels come. ~Matt Groening

What a lovely surprise to finally discover how unlonely being alone can be. ~Ellen Burstyn

Whenever I date a guy, I think, is this the man I want my children to spend their weekends with. ~Rita Rudner

My wife and I tried to breakfast together, but we had to stop or our marriage would have been wrecked. ~Winston Churchill

The secret to a happy marriage remains a secret. ~Henny Youngman

Love is temporary insanity curable by marriage. ~Ambrose Bierce

10
WORK-RELATED STRESS

With the fearful strain that is on me night and day, if I did not laugh I should die.

~Abraham Lincoln

Researchers have found that a sense of humor is one of the most commonly-possessed traits of successful business leaders. The best leaders, it turns out, are adept at using humor to cope with and overcome the inevitable stress of their roles. These are not clownish individuals; they are people who take their work, but not themselves, seriously. If employees feel free to laugh in their workplace, they too can alleviate their daily stresses and improve both their work experience and productivity.

A common goal of all businesses is to obtain and retain talented, capable employees. One way of doing that is by creating a work environment that encourages the open sharing of humor. A recent study by Yale University researchers found that depressed workers have a significantly negative impact on productivity. The study looked at 6,000 employees in three companies and found that the depressed were twice as likely to take sick days and seven times more likely to be less productive than their non-depressed coworkers. Laughter, however, improves health and increases productivity by physically relaxing people and reducing their stress levels. Laughter also strengthens bonds among coworkers by enhancing their feelings of commonality.

Dark, gallows humor is a common tension-relieving tool used in particularly stressful lines of work such as law enforcement, medicine and the social services, where tragedies of the worst kind can be witnessed on a daily basis. Without it, the individuals employed in these capacities could quickly become overwhelmed by the weight of all the horrors and suffering they see. In such cases, humor becomes not only a defense mechanism, but a survival mechanism. Without it, their work and their world could break them.

Dr. Joel Goodman of The Humor Project coined "The AT&T Principle," which states that workplace humor should be Appropriate, Timely and Tasteful. This is important to remember since humor can be divisive if it is insensitive or intentionally insulting. Whether or not your coworkers will find something funny is dependent upon a variety of variables, including their cultural background, education, intelligence, geographical location and the context. Social etiquette is as important in the use of humor as it is in other aspects of our daily interactions, and it should always be a priority in the workplace.

Paul McGhee, Ph.D., author of *Humor as a Management Tool,* identified the following ways in which humor can improve the work environment:

> *Humor can strengthen bonds between coworkers, create rapport with customers, get and hold attention, strengthen memory of the points you want to be remembered, persuade others to see (and perhaps adopt) your point of view, make awkward communications less difficult, deflect criticism, reduce tension, frustration and anger, manage conflicts, reduce burnout, remove intimidating barriers between management and non-management employees, bolster eroding trust, boost morale and motivate employees, build resilience, stimulate creative problem-solving, sustain a positive attitude on the job, and keep everyday hassles and problems in perspective.*

Management consultants are increasingly using humor as a tool in the workplace to enhance feelings of camaraderie and provide positive motivation for greater productivity and efficiency. Employers who are reluctant to embrace humorous employees due to their perceived non-serious, non-professional nature should know that many researchers have found that a sense of humor is a good indicator of intelligence. In a study conducted in 2008, Daniel Howrigan of the University of Colorado at Boulder asked subjects to write humorous statements and draw funny pictures. The subjects who scored the highest on intelligence tests were rated by observers as being significantly funnier than other subjects. By discouraging the use of humor in the workplace, employers may be unintentionally limiting the development and productivity of their most competent employees.

Whether your employer permits on-the-job joviality or not, the following sources of work-related humor can help you de-stress and decompress on your most trying days.

MOVIES FOR WORK-RELATED STRESS (Synopses courtesy of RottenTomatoes.com)

The Devil Wears Prada (Anne Hathaway, Meryl Streep and Emily Blunt)

> *Andrea is a small-town girl in her first job out of college, who tries to navigate the waters of the high-powered fashion magazine world -- while surviving her impossibly demanding new boss.*

Office Space (Ron Livingston, Jennifer Aniston and David Herman)

> *Peter Gibbons is computer programmer who at the ripe old age of 28 is having a mid-life crisis. Unable to endure another moment of the mind-numbing routine and petty annoyances that assault him day after day, Peter and some equally frustrated colleagues hatch a plot which could lead to a very lucrative and early retirement.*

Nine to Five (Dolly Parton, Jane Fonda and Lily Tomlin)

Recently divorced Judy Bernly takes an office job and soon becomes pals with fellow secretaries Violet Newstead and Doralee Rhodes. Their boss is male chauvinist Franklin Hart Jr. , who is trying to land Doralee in bed. While smoking pot one night the women hatch a plan to take revenge on their cruel boss.

Clerks (Brian O'Hallora and Jeff Anderson)

The trials and tribulations of a New Jersey convenience store clerk and his best friend, a video store employee.

Waiting (Ryan Reynolds, Justin Long and Anna Faris)

A waiter for four years since high school, Dean has never questioned his job at Shenanigan's. But when he learns that Chett, a high school classmate, now has a lucrative career in electrical engineering, he's thrown into turmoil about his dead-end life.

Broadcast News (William Hurt, Albert Brooks and Holly Hunter)

A satiric look at the inner workings of the Washington news bureau of a major TV network and the romantic triangle between the feisty young female producer, the vain male news anchor, and the good-hearted male reporter.

Working Girl (Melanie Griffith, Harrison Ford and Sigourney Weaver)

> *An ambitious secretary climbs up the corporate ladder by taking over when her boss breaks her leg.*

The Producers (Gene Wilder, Zero Mostel and Dick Shawn)

> *Producers Max Bialystock (Mostel) and Leo Bloom (Wilder) make money by producing a sure-fire flop.*

The Hudsucker Proxy (Tim Robbins, Jennifer Jason Leigh and Paul Newman)

> *Set in New York circa 1958, a man quickly climbs his way up the corporate ladder at a conglomerate after starting in the mail room. He reaches the position of chairman after the boss takes a dive out the window.*

Thank You For Smoking (Aaron Eckhart, Maria Bello and David Koechner)

> *Nick Naylor, chief spokesman for Big Tobacco, makes his living defending the rights of smokers and cigarette makers in today's neo-puritanical culture.*

BOOKS FOR WORK-RELATED STRESS

Laffirmations: 1001 Ways to Add Humor to Your Life and Work, by Joel Goodman

Claw Your Way to the Top: How to Become the Head of a Major Corporation in Roughly a Week, by Dave Barry

Straight Man: A Novel, by Richard Russo

Corporate Wildlife: The Certified Guide to Modern Office Humor, by Thejendra B. S. Sreenivas

Then We Came to the End, by Joshua Ferris

Humor as Survival Training for a Stressed-Out World: The 7 Humor Habits Program, by Paul McGhee

Post Office, by Charles Bukowski

Humor at Work: The Guaranteed, Bottom-Line, Low Cost, High-Efficiency Guide to Success Through Humor, by Esther Blumenfeld and Lynne Alpern

Relax – You May Only Have a Few Minutes Left: Using the Power of Humor to Overcome Stress in Your Life and Work, by Loretta LaRoche

Laughing Matters: The Value of Humor in the Workplace, by Ann Fry

WORK-RELATED STRESS QUOTES

If work was so good, the rich would have kept more of it for themselves. ~David Brent

I always arrive late at the office, but I make up for it by leaving early. ~Charles Lamb

In any organization there will always be one person who knows what is going on.   This person must be fired. ~Conway's Law

I am a friend of the workingman; I would rather be his friend than be one. ~Clarence Darrow

Know your limitations and be content with them. Too much ambition results in promotion to a job you can't do. ~David Brent

Success is not the key to happiness. Happiness is the key to success. If you love what you are doing, you will be successful. ~Albert Schweitzer

When a man tells you that he got rich through hard work, ask him: 'Whose?' ~Don Marquis

One of the symptoms of an approaching nervous breakdown is the belief that one's work is terribly important. ~ Bertrand Russel

The brain is a wonderful organ; it starts working the moment you get up in the morning and does not stop until you get into the office. ~Robert Frost

Lisa, if you don't like your job you don't strike. You just go in every day and do it really half-assed. That's the American way. ~Homer Simpson.

11
ILLNESS

The greatest part of our happiness depends on our
dispositions, not our circumstances.

~Martha Washington

In 2000, the Mayo Clinic reported the findings of a 30-year study in which it was discovered that optimistic people live approximately 19% longer than pessimistic people. Toshihiko Maruta, a psychiatrist and lead researcher in the study, stated, "It confirmed our common-sense belief ... and tells us that mind and body are linked and that attitude has an impact on the final outcome, death."

Optimism confers its positive benefits in much the same way as the placebo effect. Both involve the use of one's thoughts and beliefs to alter brain chemistry and induce self-healing. Most people are familiar with the placebo effect, in which the belief that a medication will be effective in the treatment of an ill is enough to make it effective, even when that "medication" is actually comprised of completely inert substances. If you have a crushing headache and I hand you a sugar pill but tell you that it is an extremely powerful painkiller, your belief in my statement alone will typically decrease activity in the pain-related regions of your brain such as the insula and cingulate gyrus. At the same time, activity will increase in the brain regions associated with mental control, the lateral and medial prefrontal regions, which are also associated with reappraisal. The anticipation of relief will lead to the imagination of relief, which will trick the mind into the experience of relief through a form of positive reappraisal. Optimists do with their positive thoughts what others do when they take a placebo -- heal themselves.

Unfortunately, the placebo effect works in the opposite direction when negative reappraisal is in effect. If a child thinks that cutting his hair will cause him pain, areas of the brain involved in the experience of pain and concomitant emotions (the cingulate gyrus and temporal regions) will become active when you approach him with scissors. Cutting his hair at this point is likely to result in tears and the perception of actual pain on his part, not to mention frustration and a belief on your part that he is merely overreacting. But bring his little brother in and show that it doesn't hurt him when his hair is cut and the child's cingulate-temporal activity will decrease, along with his pain.

These examples demonstrate the real power of mind over matter and, specifically, the power of the mind over the body. When we become ill we can tend to focus our attention on our most painful symptoms and on our fears of more significant pain and suffering. When we do this, we can unwittingly be making ourselves worse. By actively imagining and dwelling on pain and misery, we can self-induce those things and experience them as real. Dwelling on our uncomfortable and painful symptoms rarely (if ever) improves them. Focusing our attention instead on positive experiences and emotions can not only reduce the intensity of our suffering, but can sometimes, depending on the condition and its severity, eliminate it.

A good technique for remaining positive in the face of illness is to think of and visualize funny stories about things that could happen after your recovery. They can involve funny encounters with loved ones, having laughs with friends or anything else you choose to imagine. Visualizing yourself in more healthy, and specifically funny, circumstances will activate brain chemistry that will help you combat the unpleasant symptoms of your illness.

Although one never hopes for illness or suffering, most philosophers believe(d) that a fulfilling life is not possible without the periodic experience of some kind of misery. As Friedrich Nietzche famously inquired:

What if pleasure and displeasure were so tied together that whoever wanted to have as much as possible of one must also have as much as possible of the other ... you have the choice: either as little displeasure as possible, or as much displeasure as possible as the price for the growth of an abundance of subtle pleasures and joys that have rarely been relished yet? If you decide for the former and desire to diminish and lower the level of human pain, you also have to diminish and lower the level of their capacity for joy.

This is not to say that one should aspire to experience as much misery as possible as a means of getting some kind of promised joy-filled payoff later, but rather that one should take some comfort in knowing that there is more to life than the miseries that Mother Nature has bestowed upon us. Misery and pain are ultimately unavoidable, but they prime us to fully appreciate the joys and pleasures of life. The key to a fulfilling life is in learning how to not only endure the pain and suffering, but to find a way to have some fun along the way in spite of it. The following sources of humorous entertainment can help the ill gain a new perspective on their suffering while also helping them to develop the brain chemistry and internal resources to combat it.

MOVIES FOR THE ILL (Synopses courtesy of RottenTomatoes.com)

All of Me (Steve Martin, Lily Tomlin and Victoria Tennant)

> *Lily Tomlin plays a sickly spinster who is given the chance to transfer her soul to the body of another woman, and thus go on living. But the magic man who is supposed to make this happen goofs up and locks her spirit inside a bachelor lawyer (Steve Martin)--or, more accurately, within the right half of the poor fellow's body.*

What About Bob? (Bill Murray, Richard Dreyfuss and Julie Hagerty)

Egotistical New York City psychiatrist Dr. Leo Marvin is harangued and harassed by phobic patient Bob Wiley, who idolizes and worships the doctor.

Patch Adams (Robin Williams, Daniel London and Monica Potter)

Fact-based story of Hunter "Patch" Adams (Robin Williams), the founder of the Gesundheit Clinic, which deals with its patients with humor and pathos.

Benny & Joon (Johnny Depp, Mary Stuart Masterson and Aidan Quinn)

A quirky young man moves in with an overprotective mechanic and his spirited younger sister and changes their lives.

Throw Momma From The Train (Danny DeVito, Billy Crystal and Kim Greist)

Two men have someone they would dearly love dead; one his ex-wife who is making his life miserable, the other his domineering, nasty mother. What could be simpler than exchanging murders to avoid any suspicions of complicity? But Momma turns out to be a hard nut to crack.

Kingpin (Woody Harrelson, Randy Quaid and Vanessa Angel)

Roy Munson is a one-time bowling prodigy who has been reduced to scavenging for a living as a bowling supply salesman after his right hand is amputated in a bowling ball-return mechanism. Then he discovers a protege named Ishmael among the Amish of Pennsylvania Dutch Country, and the former champ thinks he has found his ticket back to the fast lane: the million dollar winner-take-all bowling tournament in Reno, Nevada.

God Said, Ha! (Julia Sweeney and Quentin Tarrantino)

"Saturday Night Live" alumna Julia Sweeney scores in a funny and moving one-woman show about a tumultuous year in her life. Her adored brother is diagnosed with cancer and takes up residence in her bedroom, and her parents move into the guestroom -- forcing Sweeney to relive her childhood in a bizarre nuclear-family flashback.

Broadway Danny Rose (Woody Allen, Mia Farrow and Nick Apollo Forte)

The career of a small-time Broadway talent agent whose roster of hopeless clients and bad luck send him on a series of adventures is recalled by some old Catskills comedians swapping tales at Jewish deli in New York.

Funny People (Adam Sandler, Seth Rogen and Leslie Mann)

> *When seasoned comedian George Simmons learns of his terminal, inoperable health condition, his desire to form a genuine friendship cause him to take a relatively green performer under his wing as his opening act.*

50 First Dates (Adam Sandler and Drew Barrymore)

> *Henry Roth is a man afraid of commitment up until he meets the beautiful Lucy. They hit it off and Henry think he's finally found the girl of his dreams, until he discovers she has short-term memory loss and forgets him the very next day.*

BOOKS FOR THE ILL

Stay Fit and Healthy Until You're Dead, by Dave Barry

The Healing Power of Humor, by Allen Klein

The Placebo Chronicles: Strange But True Tales From the Doctors' Lounge, by Douglas Farrago, M.D. and Gordon W. Marshall

The Asperger Parent: How to Raise a Child with Asperger Syndrome and Maintain Your Sense of Humor, by Jeffrey Cohen

Finding the Light in Cancer's Shadow: Hope, Humor and Healing after Treatment, by Lynn Eib

Humor and Healing, by Bernie S. Siegel, M.D.

Cancer on Five Dollars a Day (chemo not included): How Humor Got Me Through the Toughest Journey of My Life, by Robert Schimmel and Alan Eisenstock

Voices of Alzheimer's: Courage, Humor, Hope and Love In the Face of Dementia, by Betsy Peterson

Laugh! I Thought I'd Die (If I Didn't): Daily Meditations on Healing through Humor, by Anne Wilson Schaef

Gesundheit!: Bringing Good Health to You, the Medical System, and Society through Physician Service, Complementary Therapies, Humor, and Joy, by Patch Adams, M.D. and Maureen Mylander

ILLNESS-RELATED QUOTES

A good laugh and a long sleep are the best cures in the doctor's book. ~Irish Proverb

He Who Limps Is Still Walking. ~Joan Rivers

'Tis healthy to be sick sometimes. ~Henry David Thoreau

Without fear and illness, I could never have accomplished all I have. ~Edvard Munch

Warning: Humor may be hazardous to your illness. ~Ellie Katz

It's no longer a question of staying healthy. It's a question of finding a sickness you like. ~Jackie Mason

How do I stay so healthy and boyishly handsome? It's simple. I drink the blood of young runaways. ~William Shatner

The statistics on sanity are that one out of every four Americans is suffering from some form of mental illness. Think of your three best friends. If they're okay, then it's you. ~Rita Mae Brown

I assume that to prevent illness in later life, you should never have been born at all. ~George Bernard Shaw

I enjoy convalescence. It is the part that makes the illness worthwhile. ~ George Bernard Shaw.

12
FINANCIAL LOSS

You can turn painful situations around through laughter.

If you can find humor in anything, even poverty,

you can survive it.

~Bill Cosby

Department of Labor statistics indicate that the average man in his mid-thirties in 2007 earned 12% less than his father did thirty years ago, adjusted for inflation. Globalization, outsourcing and the most recent economic crisis have all contributed to a significant decline in personal income with no solution in sight. Millions of people have experienced significant loss of money, loss of social standing and poverty in recent years, and the adjustment can be a difficult one.

In the United States where much of the population is perpetually preoccupied with "keeping up with the

Joneses," and striving for status, the current state of financial affairs is delivering a particularly painful blow. Advertising executives and masters of marketing have spent billions of dollars convincing us that our self worth is directly related to what we own. In many ways, our possessions have come to represent who we are and we often value them as extensions of ourselves. Do you think more highly of someone if they drive a Bentley than if they drive a Toyota Tercel? The person in the Tercel could be devoting their life to saving children from abusive homes while the person in the Bentley could be a drug kingpin, but we have been trained by marketing gurus to judge books by their covers rather than their content, so we automatically confer more positive traits on the Bentley driver than the Tercel driver.

There is no scientific evidence that indicates that Bentley drivers are more virtuous and valuable people than Tercel drivers, but we believe it because we have been inundated with such messages by advertisers since birth. This creates a problem when forces beyond our control require us to downgrade our possessions and sacrifice the prestige that comes with them. There is a real sense of loss -- not just of the objects, but of our sense of personal worth. To change this situation and regain some of our lost self-respect, we do not need to strive to earn more money so we can go on spending sprees to refill our self-esteem tanks; we simply need to reexamine and readjust our views and beliefs about the true meaning and purpose of these possessions.

Henry David Thoreau wisely said, "That man is richest whose pleasures are cheapest." Philosophers through the ages have repeatedly pronounced that the simple things in life provide as much, if not more, pleasure and happiness as the so-called "best" things. Have you ever been eating at a fine restaurant in your finest of finery and had the thought that you would rather be at home eating popcorn in bed and watching a movie? That is just one example of how the simple and less expensive can trump the extravagant and more expensive. We often dismiss the simple pleasures as pedestrian or beneath us because the advertisers want us to -- they want us to spend money on their pricey products instead. But philosophers are the ultimate truth-seekers and gain nothing in deception, so their words and observations should carry a little more weight than that high-end car commercial or that ad for a $1,000 pair of shoes.

Humor is a good place to start to not only recalibrate our values and get back to the simple pleasures, but to readjust our perceptions about the true worth of our things and ourselves. When we do this, we find that our possessions and social status do not determine our happiness and value -- we do.

When the stock market is crashing, when your boss has handed you a pink slip or when some other misfortune has brought your capacity to gather possessions down a notch, do not dwell on the loss. Turn your thoughts instead to what stands to be gained; specifically, discovery of more simple pleasures and joys that you had previously been overlooking or taking for granted. The following loss-related humorous sources are a good place to begin that discovery process.

MOVIES FOR FINANCIAL LOSS (Synopses courtesy of RottenTomatoes.com)

The Big Lebowski (Jeff Bridges and John Goodman)

> *A pothead bowler who is mistaken for a deadbeat philanthropist is drawn into a cluster of kidnappers, nihilists, porn mobsters and Busby Berkeley beauties.*

Fun With Dick and Jane (Jim Carrey and Téa Leoni)

> *Dick Harper's years of hard work finally pay off when he is promoted to vice president at Globodyne, a worldwide leader in the consolidation of media properties. But, after exactly one day in his new job, Globodyne is destroyed by an Enron-like calamity -- and he is left holding the bag.*

Envy (Jack Black and Ben Stiller)

> *When Nick (Jack Black) invents an aerosol spray that makes dog-poop disappear, he reaps a fortune overnight and sends his friend, co-worker and neighbor Tim (Ben Stiller) into a tailspin of simmering envy, since he had no faith in Nick's get-rich-quick scheme and declined his offer of 50-50 partnership.*

Trading Places (Dan Aykroyd and Eddie Murphy)

> *The fabulously wealthy but morally bankrupt Duke brothers make a one-dollar bet over heredity vs. environment. Curious as to what would happen if different lifestyles were reversed, they arrange for*

impoverished street hustler Billy Ray Valentine to be placed in the lap of luxury. Simultaneously, they strip wealthy Louis Winthorpe III of his identity and wealth.

The Full Monty (Robert Carlyle, Mark Addy and William Snape)

Set in the British steel town of Sheffield, a group of out-of-work steel workers are organized by fun loving, slightly irresponsible Gaz into a Chippendale-style dance troupe.

You Can't Take It With You (James Stewart, Jean Arthur and Lionel Barrymore)

This is the story of the zany Sycamore household, presided over by Grandpa Vanderhof (Lionel Barrymore), a former businessman who has turned his back on commerce to enjoy life. At the Sycamores', everyone does just what he or she pleases.

Zack and Miri Make a Porno (Seth Rogen and Elizabeth Banks)

Lifelong friends Zack and Miri look to solve their cash flow problems by recruiting a motley cast and crew to make an adult film. As the cameras roll, the duo discovers unexpected romantic feelings for each other.

Dumb and Dumber (Jim Carrey and Jeff Daniels)

> *Two underachievers follow the girl of their dreams to Aspen, Colorado to return her lost briefcase.*

Take the Money and Run (Woody Allen and Janet Margolin)

> *This side-splitting takeoff of crime documentaries stars Allen as Virgil Starkwell, a sweetly inept career criminal.*

Joe Dirt (David Spade and Brittany Daniel)

> *David Spade stars as Joe Dirt, an idiot who works as an oil weller who is on the search for his parents who abandoned him at the Grand Canyon when he was a baby.*

BOOKS FOR FINANCIAL LOSS

Slow Love: How I Lost My Job, Put on My Pajamas & Found Happiness, by Dominique Browning

The Queen and I, by Sue Townsend

Dave Barry's Money Secrets, by Dave Barry

Cold Comfort Farm, by Stella Gibbons

Sellevision, by Augusten Burroughs

Fat, Forty, Fired: One Man's Frank, Funny, and Inspiring Account of Losing His Job and Finding His Life, by Nigel Marsh

Syrup, by Maxx Barry

Enderby Outside, by Anthony Burgess

Vanity Fire, by John M. Daniel

And I Shall Have Some Peace There: Trading in the Fast Lane for My Own Dirt Road, by Margaret Roach

FINANCIAL LOSS-RELATED QUOTES

There is no defense against adverse fortune which is so effectual as an habitual sense of humor. ~Thomas W. Higginson

Waste your money and you're only out of money, but waste your time and you've lost a part of your life. ~Michael Leboeuf

He is rich or poor according to what he is, not according to what he has. ~Henry Ward Beecher

The essence of philosophy is that a man should so live that his happiness shall depend as little as possible on external things. ~Epictetus

Empty pockets never held anyone back. Only empty heads and empty hearts can do that. ~Norman Vincent Peale

The best way for a person to have happy thoughts is to count his blessings and not his cash. ~Author Unknown

Enough is as good as a feast. ~English Proverb

Contentment makes poor men rich; discontentment makes rich men poor. ~Benjamin Franklin

Nothing can bring you peace but yourself. ~Ralph Waldo Emerson

Another good thing about being poor is that when you are seventy your children will not have you declared legally insane in order to gain control of your estate. ~Woody Allen.

13
LOW SELF-ESTEEM

There is no cosmetic for beauty like happiness.

~Lady Blessington

Low self-esteem is a very common cause of distress and can powerfully impact the degree to which one's goals and dreams are realized. If you feel incompetent or unworthy, you are not likely to seek or pursue high aspirations. Failing to pursue higher aspirations, in turn, further reduces your self-esteem by limiting one of its primary sources -- that of accomplishment. What you believe to be true about yourself will dictate who you are and what you do in the world. If what you believe is negative and not in line with reality, you will consistently sell yourself short and live a less satisfying life than you could and should.

The operative word here is "believe," because so much of what we think about ourselves is based on belief rather than on fact. Perfectionists and people who come from abusive or neglectful backgrounds are at particular risk for developing low self-esteem and suffering from its adverse consequences. They tend to focus on, and place greater emphasis on, their flaws and mistakes rather than on their strengths and successes. Sometimes this occurs as a result of being repeatedly denigrated by others or being told that their best is not good enough. They eventually internalize the outside sources that originally delivered these messages, and these become the dominant voices in their minds. What they often fail to consider is the degree to which those who originally delivered these messages are flawed themselves.

Every single person on the planet is flawed in some way or another, seen or unseen, and some people point out the flaws of others to detract from or minimize their own. These people induce unwarranted low self-esteem in their targets if the targets accept and dwell on their criticisms. The key to avoiding self-loathing is to accept criticism, but not dwell on and drown in it. Accept that you are indeed not perfect and that you probably never will be, and know that no one is all bad, all good or close to perfect. Use your energy to focus on your better qualities and strengths and expand upon them. Your flaws will be minimized in the process and your self-esteem will grow.

When you take in criticism from others and allow it to define your being, you are giving those people control over your life and your happiness. At some point you have to decide that it is your life and that you alone will determine its value and direction.

Writer Ramona L. Anderson said, "People spend a lifetime searching for happiness; looking for peace. They chase idle dreams, addictions, religions, even other people, hoping to fill the emptiness that plagues them. The irony is the only place they ever needed to search was within." We are all influenced tremendously by the outside world and social forces beyond our control, but our power to define ourselves is far greater than that of anyone or anything external. What we choose to believe and where we choose to focus our attention are the most powerful determinants of who we are and who we become. The idle opinions of outsiders only affect us if we permit them to. The key to raising one's self-esteem is to stop placing so much weight on those opinions.

Your flaws are like a sharp pebble in your shoe. As you walk along the road of life, you can continually grind your foot into the pebble as a constant reminder that it is there, and ultimately develop a sore and possible life-threatening infection. Or you can acknowledge that the pebble is there and favor your other pebble-free foot so that you experience as little damage and pain as possible. The choice of which foot to favor is not the pebble's and it is not the outside world's -- it is yours alone. You, and only you, are in control of the effect, even if you are not in control of the cause.

Of course, we should always strive to be better people and work to overcome our flaws; but as long as we are doing the best we can and not hurting others, we should not endlessly punish ourselves for having them.

The sources of humor on the following pages will help you begin to recognize the universality of human imperfection, and will challenge your self-limiting thoughts and beliefs.

MOVIES FOR LOW SELF-ESTEEM (Synopses courtesy of RottenTomatoes.com)

Raising Arizona (Nicolas Cage and Holly Hunter)

> *A petty crook falls in love with the female cop who always arrests him, but when they find out she can't bear children, they steal one, hit the road, and lots of mayhem ensues.*

Little Miss Sunshine (Abigail Breslin, Greg Kinnear and Toni Collette)

> *The Hoover family treks from Albuquerque to the Little Miss Sunshine pageant in Redondo Beach, California, to fulfill the deepest wish of 7-year-old Olive, an ordinary little girl with big dreams. Along the way the family must deal with crushed dreams, heartbreaks and a broken-down VW bus.*

Annie Hall (Woody Allen and Diane Keaton)

> *"Annie Hall" is a comical look at the up and down relationship between a New York City TV writer and his aspiring actress/singer girlfriend who's originally from the Midwest.*

The 40 Year Old Virgin (Steve Carell and Catherine Keener)

Andy Stitzer is a nice guy. He's shy, considerate, polite, lives alone, rides his bicycle to work at Circuit City, has a pristine collection of action figures, is pathologically nervous around women and at 40 years old, is still a virgin. When his co-workers discover this, they make it their mission to get Andy laid.

Best In Show (Fred Willard, Eugene Levy and Catherine O'Hara)

A "behind the scenes" look into the highly competitive and cut-throat world of dog-shows through the eyes of a group of ruthless dog owners.

Miss Firecracker (Holly Hunter, Mary Steenburgen and Tim Robbins)

Carnelle isn't happy with her life, so in order to improve herself she enters a local beauty contest, trying to emulate her cousin Elain's win many years ago. Few think she can win, even her closest friends and relatives, but Carnelle is ever hopeful, seeing a win as a ticket to escape her small town in Mississippi.

Harold and Kumar Go To White Castle (John Cho, Ethan Embry and Robert Tinkler)

Two likeable underdogs, Harold and Kumar, set out on a Friday night quest to satisfy their craving for White Castle hamburgers and end up on an epic journey of deep thoughts and a wild road trip.

For Your Consideration (Catherine O'Hara, Harry Shearer and Parker Posey)

> *Debut feature director Jay Berman steers cast and crew through a typically tumultuous independent film "Home for Purim," an intimate period drama about a Jewish family's turbulent reunion on the occasion of the dying matriarch's favorite holiday. When (erroneous) Internet-generated rumors begin circulating that three of the film's stars are generating Oscar buzz, a rumble of excitement rattles the quirky cast.*

Being There (Peter Sellers, Shirley MacLaine and Melvyn Douglas)

> *Chance, a simple gardener, has never left the estate until his employer dies. His simple TV-informed utterances are mistaken for profundity.*

My Cousin Vinny (Joe Pesci, Marisa Tomei and Ralph Macchio)

> *Bill and Stan are mistaken for murderers while on vacation, and Bill's family sends his cousin to defend them for his first case as a lawyer.*

BOOKS FOR LOW SELF-ESTEEM

How I Got to be Perfect, by Jean Kerr

The Complete Stories of Dorothy Parker, by Dorothy Parker

Me Talk Pretty One Day by David Sedaris

Confederacy of Dunces, by John Kennedy Toole

Diary of an Emotional Idiot: A Novel, by Maggie Estep

Coming to Terms with Mediocrity: And Other Humorous Life Lessons, by Kari Breed

Scoop, by Evelyn Waugh

Diary of a Mad Fat Girl, by Stephanie McAfee

Small Medium at Large: How to Develop a Powerful Verbal Sense of Humor, by Paul E. McGhee

Lucky Jim, by Kingsley Amis

LOW SELF-ESTEEM QUOTES

Low self-esteem is like driving through life with your hand-break on. ~Maxwell Maltz

Good judgment comes from experience, and a lot of that comes from bad judgment. ~Will Rogers

All the things I really like are either immoral, illegal or fattening. ~Alexander Woollcott

I'd rather be a failure at something I love than a success at something I hate. ~George Burns

If you're not failing every now and again, it's a sign you're not doing anything very innovative. ~Woody Allen

It's not what I do, but the way I do it. It's not what I say, but the way I say it ~Mae West

I've often said, the only thing standing between me and greatness is me. ~Woody Allen

Never think that you're not good enough yourself. A man should never think that. People will take you very much at your own reckoning ~Anthony Trollope

You tried your best and you failed miserably. The lesson is 'never try'. ~Homer Simpson

Rarely is the question asked: Is our children learning? ~George W. Bush.

14
ANGER

You get tragedy where the tree, instead of bending, breaks.

~Ludwig Wittgenstein

From road-ragers to violent parents at children's sporting events to girl-fighters on YouTube to high school students who kill and beyond, there are endless numbers of angry people in the world who are wreaking havoc with their rage at any given moment. Anger is the source of a tremendous amount of suffering, but it does not have to be. It is an emotion that can be controlled with better knowledge of its functioning and the use of techniques that minimize its impact.

Neuroscientist Golnaz Tabibnia of UCLA found that our emotional responses can be tempered if we identify and label the emotions we are experiencing. His research involved the study of the amygdala, the brain region responsible for alerting us to threats in our environment and inducing us to take action against those threats. Tabibnia found that, although seeing photos of angry faces elicited an emotional response from the amygdala of subjects, the intensity of the response decreased when the subjects labeled the faces as angry. The reason for this is that the process of labeling activates the linguistic centers in the prefrontal cortex, which decreases the amygdala response. Tabibnia concluded, "The prefrontal cortex attenuates responses in the brain's emotion centers. That's why emotion-labeling may help reduce emotional responses in the long term." Simply acknowledging one's angry feelings and labeling them as such will begin the process of controlling them. Although we are all born with differing emotional tendencies, emotion regulation is a learnable skill and one that can be particularly useful to the angry among us.

Once we have acknowledged that we are angry, the next step is to find ways to mitigate it. The use of humor is a good option. In *Jokes and Their Relationship to the Unconscious*, Freud wrote, "A joke will allow us to explore something ridiculous in our enemy which we could not, on account of obstacles in the way, bring forward openly or consciously." Thinking of your enemy or the object of your anger in a humorous way can often diminish the intensity of your negative feelings.

To become more adept in the use of humor, try joining an improvisation or sketch comedy class. You will learn how to be more observant, flexible and quick on your feet. If you have a funny or interesting story to tell about a particular piece of clothing or accessory, wear or carry that item with the story at-the-ready for the moment when anger threatens to overcome you. Such a humorous distraction can save the day. Opportunities for daily humorous engagement abound if you look for them and open yourself up to them. Doing so will make you happier, healthier and less prone to angry outbursts. Organizations such as Laughter for a Change (www.laughterforachange.org) offer professional -level improv classes to the public and are a great resource for those who struggle with emotional expression or social interaction.

We all can become justifiably angry when insulted or mistreated, but that does not mean that we have to react in an angry or violent manner. Humor presents a more advanced and less dangerous option. While questioning Supreme Court nominee Elena Kagan about her views on the war on terror in June 2010, Republican Senator Lindsey Graham asked where she was the previous Christmas when a group of suspected terrorists tried to blow up a Detroit-bound plane. Kagan responded, "You know, like all Jews, I was probably in a Chinese restaurant." The senators in the hearing room all laughed, including Graham, and Kagan moved a step closer to becoming the next Supreme Court Justice. She could have responded with indignation and offense, but her use of humor diffused an otherwise tense situation in which Republicans were attempting to elicit responses that would portray her as being outside the legal mainstream.

President Abraham Lincoln was another person who was adept at using humor to disarm and engage the opposition. When an opponent accused him of being two-faced, his response was: "If I were two-faced, would I be wearing this one?" As Kagan and Lincoln both recognized, humor can be a powerful social lubricant --

smoothing out the inevitable bumps that come with social interaction.

Humor can, of course, be used in aggressive and hostile ways that can actually exacerbate angry encounters. Comedian Michael Richards of *Seinfeld* fame demonstrated this fact in 2006 when he spewed racial epithets at an African American heckler during his stand-up routine at the Laugh Factory in Hollywood. The video seen around the world showed Richards repeatedly calling the man the "n-word" and making references to lynching and other civil rights abuses. The crowd's laughter tapered off as they realized that Richards' anger had overwhelmed his humor and that what they were witnessing was far from funny. One of the most interesting aspects of this story is that Michael Richards was not a racist man and had no history of ever endorsing the statements that flew from his mouth. His fury and rage overwhelmed him and he instinctively reached for whatever weapons he could find to attack the source of his anger. In the process, he mortified not only the crowd, but himself.

Anger is an extremely powerful emotion and can make us all do and say things we regret; things we would never dream of doing or saying in a non-angry state. The anger is temporary but, as Michael Richards discovered, the regret can last forever. When using humor to diffuse hostile situations, it is important to remain cognizant of the fact that your words could actually make the situation worse if you allow your anger to drive them. When your aim is to hurt the other person rather than to make light of the situation, serious consequences can result.

The following sources of humorous entertainment will challenge your angry thoughts and feelings and help you begin to replace them with more positive, productive ones.

MOVIES FOR ANGER (Synopses courtesy of RottenTomatoes.com)

Punch-Drunk Love (Adam Sandler, Don McManus and Emily Watson)

> *A beleaguered small-business owner gets a harmonium and embarks on a romantic journey with a mysterious woman.*

O Brother Where Art Thou (George Clooney, John Goodman and John Turturro)

> *In the Depression-era deep South, three escapees from a Mississippi prison chain gang: Everett Ulysses McGill, sweet and simple Delmar, and the perpetually angry Pete, embark on the adventure of a lifetime as they set out to pursue their freedom and return to their homes.*

Blazing Saddles (Mel Brooks and Gene Wilder)

> *When the new railroad is scheduled to go through the frontier town of Rock Ridge, corrupt State Attorney General Hedley Lamarr sends thugs to scare the townspeople off the newly valuable land so he can buy it himself.*

As Good As It Gets (Jack Nicholson, Helen Hunt and Greg Kinnear)

> *An obsessive-compulsive curmudgeon (Jack Nicholson) develops a more positive outlook as a result of his interactions with his gay neighbor (Greg Kinnear) and an optimistic waitress (Helen Hunt).*

I Love You, Man (Paul Rudd, Jon Favreau and Jason Segal)

> *A successful real estate agent, who upon getting engaged to the woman of his dreams, Zooey, discovers, to his dismay and chagrin, that he has no male friend close enough to serve as his Best Man. Peter immediately sets out to rectify the situation, embarking on a series of bizarre and awkward "man-dates."*

Talladega Nights: The Ballad of Ricky Bobby (Will Ferrell, John C. Reilly and Sacha Baron Cohen)

> *Ricky Bobby is a go-for-broke race car driver who, in races, either finishes first or doesn't finish at all. Unhappy with these results, Bobby's team owner brings over Jean Girard, a French Formula One driver, who quickly becomes Bobby's biggest rival.*

Stir Crazy (Gene Wilder and Richard Pryor)

> *Skip and Harry are framed for a bank robbery and end up in a western prison. The two eastern boys are having difficulty adjusting to the new life until the warden finds that Skip has a natural talent for riding broncos with the inter-prison rodeo coming up.*

Austin Powers: International Man of Mystery (Mike Myers, Elizabeth Hurley and Mimi Rogers)

> *A 1960's hipster secret agent is brought out of cryofreeze to oppose his greatest enemy into the 1990's where his social attitudes are glaringly out of place.*

The Pink Panther (David Niven, Peter Sellers and Robert Wagner)

> *In the first movie starring Peter Sellers as the bumbling Inspector Clouseau, he tries to catch a jewel thief who is right under his nose.*

Walk Hard: The Dewey Cox Story (John C. Reilly, Jenna Fischer and Raymond J. Barry)

> *Singer Dewey Cox overcomes adversity to become a musical legend.*

BOOKS FOR ANGER

The Comic Toolbox: How to Be Funny Even If You're Not, by John Vorhaus

I Am America (And So Can You!), by Stephen Colbert

The 7 ½ Habits of Highly Humorous People, by David M. Jacobson, MSW, LCSW

The Sot-Weed Factor, by John Barth

Mama, Get the Hammer! There's a Fly on Papa's Head!: Using Humor to Flatten Out Your Pain, by Barbara Johnson

Three Men in a Boat, by Jerome K. Jerome

Still Life with Woodpecker, by Tom Robbins

Sick Puppy, by Carl Hiaasen

In Fifty Years We'll All Be Chicks: … And Other Complaints from an Angry Middle-Aged White Guy, by Adam Carolla

Finding the Funny Fast: How to Create Quick Humor to Connect with Clients, Coworkers and Crowds, by Jan McInnis

ANGER-RELATED QUOTES

For every minute you are angry, you lose sixty seconds of happiness. ~Ralph Waldo Emerson

I think the next best thing to solving a problem is finding some humor in it. *~Frank Howard Clark*

Resentment is like taking poison and waiting for the other person to die. ~Malachy McCourt

Speak when you are angry and you will make the best speech you will ever regret. ~Ambrose Bierce

It's practically impossible to look at a penguin and feel angry. ~Joe Moore

People who fly into a rage always make a bad landing.
~Will Rogers

If a small thing has the power to make you angry,
does that not indicate something about your size?"
~Sydney J. Harris

My uncle Sammy was an angry man. He had printed on
his tombstone: What are you looking at? ~Margaret
Smith

How much more grievous are the consequences of anger
than the causes of it. ~Marcus Aurelius

Expressing anger is a form of public littering. ~Willard
Gaylin.

15
AGING

If you live to the age of a hundred you have it made because very few people die past the age of a hundred.

~George Burns

It has often been said that "getting old isn't for wimps" because of the physical and mental challenges that develop as we age. Not all age-related changes are bad, however. In *The Secret Life of the Grown-up Brain: The Surprising Talents of the Middle-Aged Mind,* journalist Barbara Strauch cites studies that found that the amount of myelin in the brain (the fatty substance that insulates nerve fibers) continues to increase well into middle age, boosting brain cells' processing capacity. The findings of these studies and an abundance of new research in the field indicate that, contrary to popular belief and stereotypes, the human brain hits its prime when the owner is between their early 40s and late 60s.

With age we gain new perspective and greater understanding of ourselves and the world in which we live. How many times have we said or heard someone say, "If I only knew then what I know now..."? Knowledge is power, and as we grow older we have the capacity and opportunity to gain both. As an example of the way that time and aging confer knowledge and power, try this exercise: Imagine that you can go back in time and visit yourself when you were 13-years-old. Knowing what you know now, if you could tell your 13-year-old self only one thing, what would it be? Really give it some thought before finally answering. Most people over age 30 will find that they could tell themselves some life-changing things; things that they could not have conceived or fully understood at 13.

What we lose in physical capabilities as we age, we gain in other areas that may not be so readily apparent. In our society, we celebrate youth and superficial beauty rather than experience and true substance, but that does not make youth a superior state of being. As we age we gain a better understanding of the deeper meaning in life and what is and is not important. We become more adept at judging people and situations and determining the best course of action to take. We strengthen our bonds with those who have shared our lives and experiences, and the intensity of our friendships deepens.

Despite the advantages of aging, many of us still dwell more on the negative aspects than the positive. This is why anti-aging products and plastic surgery are so common and sought-after. We are so used to the different advantages conferred by youth that we become reluctant to give them up and discover the benefits of aging. This is unfortunate because it leaves many people clinging to remnants of what they once had rather than recognizing the value of what they have now.

Neuroscientists have found that when our brains age we gain a greater capacity for recognizing patterns, making connections and being creative. The Seattle Longitudinal Study tracked 6,000 people for over 40 years and recorded their mental capabilities as they aged. The researchers discovered that subjects performed better in middle age than they did in early adulthood when tested for inductive reasoning, spatial orientation and vocabulary. Researchers in the field have found that although speed and memory decline with age, experience frequently makes up for those losses. This is especially important in areas of life that require knowledge and judgment. For example, who would you rather have flying your plane, a 55-year-old experienced pilot or a 25-year-old novice?.

Dwelling on what is lost with aging prevents us from discovering and fully embracing what is gained. The following sources of aging-related humor can be very useful in opening our eyes to the lighter, and brighter, side of growing older.

MOVIES ABOUT AGING (Synopses courtesy of RottenTomatoes.com)

The Big Chill (William Hurt, Kevin Kline and Meg Tilly)

> *A group of seven former college friends gather for a weekend reunion at a posh South Carolina winter house after the funeral of one of their friends.*

Step Brothers (John C. Reilly, Will Ferrell and Mary Steenburgen)

> *Two spoiled 40 year-old men (Ferrell and Reilly) become competitive stepbrothers after their single parents get married.*

Greenberg (Ben Stiller, Greta Gerwig and Jennifer Jason Leigh)

> *Roger Greenberg (Ben Stiller), single, fortyish and at a crossroads in his life, finds himself in Los Angeles, house-sitting for six weeks for his more successful/married-with-children brother. In search of a place to restart his life, Greenberg tries to reconnect with old friends.*

Grumpy Old Men (Jack Lemmon, Walter Matthau and Ann Margret)

> *Jack Lemmon and Walter Matthau play John and Max (respectively), a pair of elderly bachelors whose lifelong friendship is based on mutual aggravation and constant bickering. Their competitive natures kick into overdrive when the beautiful Ariel (Ann-Margret) moves into their otherwise snowbound Minnesota neighborhood.*

About Schmidt (Jack Nicholson, Hope Davis and Kathy Bates)

> *Warren Schmidt is a retired insurance salesman, who at age 66 has no particular plans other than to drive around in the motor home his wife insisted they buy. When she suddenly dies, he sets out to postpone the imminent marriage of his daughter to a man he doesn't like, while coping with discoveries about his late wife and himself in the process.*

Grown Ups (Adam Sandler, Steve Buscemi and Jamie Chung)

> *Thirty years after their high school graduation, five good friends reunite for a Fourth of July holiday weekend.*

Hot Tub Time Machine (John Cusack, Rob Corddry and Craig Robinson)

> *Hot Tub Time Machine follows a group of best friends who've become bored with their adult lives. After a crazy night of drinking in a ski resort hot tub, the men wake up, heads pounding, in the year 1986. This is their chance to kick some past and change their futures.*

Death Becomes Her (Meryl Streep, Bruce Willis and Goldie Hawn)

When a woman learns of an immortality treatment, she sees it as a way to outdo her long-time rival.

The Hammer (Adam Carolla, Oswaldo Castillo and Heather Juergensen)

A once-promising amateur boxer, 40 year-old Jerry Ferro has been knocking around from one construction job to another and spinning his wheels in an unsatisfying relationship. When a venerable boxing coach convinces Jerry that it's time to make his return to competitive boxing, Jerry ends his 20-year layoff and begins a hilarious fish-out-water quest for Olympic gold.

Old School (Will Ferrell, Luke Wilson and Vince Vaughn)

A trio of thirty-something buddies tries to recapture the outrageous, irrepressible fun of their college years by starting their own off-campus frat house.

BOOKS ABOUT AGING

This Is Getting Old: Zen Thoughts on Aging with Humor and Dignity by Susan Ichi Su Moon

The Leisure Seeker: A Novel, by Michael Zadoorian

Dave Barry Turns 40, by Dave Barry

Sh*t My Dad Says, by Justin Halpern

Humor Me, I'm Over the Hill, by Barbara Johnson

Changing Shoes: Getting Older – Not Old – with Style, Humor, and Grace, by Tina Sloan

What No One Tells the Mom: Surviving the Early Years of Parenthood with your Sanity, Your Sex Life and Your Sense of Humor Intact, by Marg Stark

Life Continues: Facing the Challenges of MS, Menopause & Midlife with Hope, Courage & Humor, by Carmen Ambrosio

Hot Flashes and Cold Cream, by Diann Hunt

The Joys of Aging – and How to Avoid Them, by Phyllis Diller

AGING-RELATED QUOTES

I don't feel old -- I don't feel anything until noon. Then it's time for my nap. ~Bob Hope

Gray hair is God's graffiti. ~Bill Cosby

Old age isn't so bad when you consider the alternatives. ~Maurice Chevalier (on his 77th birthday)

Remember that age and treachery will always triumph over youth and ability. ~David Brent

Being seventy has its advantages. I was outspoken before, but now what have I got to keep quiet about? ~Kirk Douglas

The secret of staying young is to live honestly, eat slowly and lie about your age. ~Lucille Ball

You're never too old to become younger. ~Mae West

At twenty years of age, the will reigns; at thirty the wit; at forty the judgment. ~Benjamin Franklin

I'm at the age where food has taken the place of sex in my life. In fact, I've just had a mirror put over my kitchen table. ~Rodney Dangerfield

To be seventy years young is sometimes far more cheerful and hopeful than to be forty years old. ~Oliver Wendell Holmes.

16
DEATH

There are worse things in life than death. Have you ever spent

an evening with an insurance salesman?

~Woody Allen

One of the many things that all humans share is that none of us will have a happy ending. All of our endings will be the same -- death. Conscious awareness of this fact leads to a tremendous amount of despair and philosophizing about the meaning of it all. But we can have a happy beginning, middle and everything else that occurs before the end, even if we cannot control our ultimate fate. Dwelling on death will not change its inevitability, and the time is more wisely spent enhancing our existence.

The Dalai Lama said, "Impermanence and compassion are interlinked. It is easier to arouse compassion toward the suffering of others by thinking about the transitoriness of their lives." Knowledge of our impending death and that of others makes us aware of our shared vulnerabilities and creates an impetus for deeper connection and understanding. One of the ways in which we make our time in the world more meaningful is by helping others in need and contributing in some way to the lives of future generations. In some ways, our acute awareness of our impending demise makes us become better people than we may otherwise be. And by helping others we help ourselves since few things bring as much pleasure and satisfaction as relieving the suffering of another.

Herbert Lefcourt, author of *Humor: The Psychology of Living Buoyantly,* found that the willingness of people to sign an organ donor consent form increases with their tendency to laugh. He concluded, "Very few people are ready to think, even for a moment, about death. But those who have a sense of humor are more able to cope with the idea." Humor provides a low-stress way of coming to terms with something that many find overwhelming to contemplate; and those who use it display the kind of compassion that the Dalai Lama referenced in his comment about impermanence. We cannot "beat" death in the conventional sense by never dying, but we can beat the adverse effects that our knowledge of it has upon us if we open ourselves up to laughing about it.

An important thing to bear in mind when thinking about our mortality is that there is nothing in death that is as painful as what we are capable of experiencing in life. Although many people do believe in a physical post-death hell, numerous philosophers have theorized that we are already in it -- that life is hell. The pain, suffering and horrors that humans endure in life frequently match or exceed the descriptions of those in the biblical hell. The fact of the matter is, there are worse things than dying and there are better things than dwelling on it.

Life and the contemplation of death can be hell, but it can also be made to be more like heaven if we consciously make an effort to change our outlook and focus on the good and the amusing rather than on the bad and the depressing. It is a quality of life issue that we all have more control over than we often realize. The following death-themed humor sources will help you begin to make that change in thinking and develop a new perspective on death, life and the meaning of it all.

MOVIES ABOUT DEATH (Synopses courtesy of RottenTomatoes.com)

Bucket List (Jack Nicholson, Morgan Freeman and Sean Hayes)

> *Corporate billionaire Edward Cole and working class mechanic Carter Chambers are worlds apart. At a crossroads in their lives, they share a hospital room and discover they have two things in common: a desire to spend the time they have left doing everything they ever wanted to do before they "kick the bucket" and an unrealized need to come to terms with who they are. Together they embark on the road trip of a lifetime.*

The End (Burt Reynolds, Dom DeLuise and Sally Field)

> *"Sonny" Lawson (Burt Reynolds) is informed by his doctor that he only has six months to live. Not wanting to endure the inevitable pain, nor wanting to spend his last days in a hospital bed, he decides to take his own life. After a failed suicide attempt, Lawson ends up at a psychiatric hospital. There he befriends a very disturbed fellow patient, Marlon Borunki (Dom DeLuise), who agrees to help in Sonny's quest to end it all.*

Dream With The Fishes (David Arquette and Brad Hunt)

> *Terry (David Arquette) really does want to die and Nick (Brad Hunt) really does have only a few weeks to live. The men live in the same San Francisco neighborhood, but Terry is a depressed widower, while Nick may be terminally ill, yet he and his tattoo artist girlfriend, Liz, live life to the fullest.*

Changing Hearts (Faye Dunaway, Lauren Holly and Tom Skerritt)

> *Two women, Betty (Faye Dunaway) and Amber (Lauren Holly), become special friends with a strong, unshakable bond when they're both diagnosed with breast cancer. In addition to their shared malady, the two companions -- to keep their spirits up -- also dish about the men with whom they've recently been involved.*

Defending Your Life (Albert Brooks, Michael Durrell and James Eckhouse)

> *The first true story about the afterlife.*

Harold and Maude (Ruth Gordon, Bud Cort and Vivian Pickles)

> *Young, rich, and obsessed with death, Harold finds himself changed forever when he meets lively septuagenarian Maude at a funeral.*

The Barbarian Invasions (Rémy Girard, Dorothée Berryman and Stéphane Rousseau)

> *Rémy, divorced and in his early fifties, is hospitalized. His ex-wife, Louise, asks their son Sébastien to come home from London where he now lives. As soon as he arrives, Sébastien reunites the merry band of folk who were all players in Rémy's complicated past: relatives, friends and former mistresses.*

Kiss Me Goodbye (Sally Field, James Caan and Jeff Bridges)

> *Sally Field is a woman about to embark on her second marriage after her first husband, a charismatic Broadway director and choreographer (James Caan), has died. But as she plans her wedding to the likable but unexciting Jeff Bridges, Caan returns from the*

dead. Though only she can see him, it's a formula for disaster.

Parting Shots (Chris Rea and Felicity Kendal)

Harry Sterndale, a failed photographer, is told that he has cancer and has only three months to live. He decides that since he is dying anyway he will kill or destroy all the people who have ever crossed or hurt him.

Two Weeks (Sally Field, Ben Chaplin and Julianne Nicholson)

Four siblings rush home to say a last goodbye to their very sick mother. When she hangs on, they find themselves trapped together for two weeks.

BOOKS ABOUT DEATH

The Courage to Laugh, by Allen Klein

Famous Last Words and Tombstone Humor, by Gyles Brandreth

Mort, by Terry Pratchett

Of Corpse: Death and Humor in Folklore and Popular Culture, by Peter Narvaez

A Dirty Job, by Christopher Moore

The Definitive Guide to Underground Humor: Quaint Quotes About Death, Funny Funeral Home Stories and Hilarious Headstone Epitaphs, by Edward Bergin

Sex, Death and Fly Fishing, by John Gierach

Good Omens, by Terry Pratchett and Neil Gaiman

Wit and Wisdom for Widows: Beginning Anew, by Barbara Whitman Gaeta and Susan Whitman

Death: A Life, by George Pendle

DEATH-RELATED QUOTES

It's not that I'm afraid to die. I just don't want to be there when it happens ~Woody Allen

Drink and dance and laugh and lie, love the reeling midnight through, for tomorrow we shall die (but alas we never do)! ~Dorothy Parker

In the creation of comedy, it is paradoxical that tragedy stimulates the spirit of ridicule, because ridicule, I suppose, is an attitude of defiance; we must laugh in the face of our helplessness against the forces of nature -- or go insane. ~Charlie Chaplin

I know this will come as a shock to you, Mr. Goldwyn, but in all history, which has held billions and billions of human beings, not a single one ever had a happy ending. ~Dorothy Parker

There is nothing dreadful in life to the man who has truly comprehended that there is nothing terrible in not living. ~Epicurus

Don't think of death as an ending. Think of it as a really effective way of cutting down your expenses. ~Woody Allen

I do not believe in an afterlife, although I am bringing a change of underwear. ~Woody Allen

The fear of death is the most unjustified of all fears, for there's no risk of accident for someone who's dead. ~Albert Einstein.

According to most studies, people's number one fear is public speaking. Number two is death. Death is number two! Does that sound right? This means to the average person, if you go to a funeral, you're better off in the casket than doing the eulogy. ~Jerry Seinfeld

If life must not be taken too seriously, then so neither must death. ~Samuel Butler.

CONCLUSION

Researchers have repeatedly and consistently demonstrated the therapeutic value of humor, and the humorous sources recommended herein are a fun and effective way to begin realizing those benefits. Throughout this book were quotes from philosophers, scientists, artists, authors, intellectuals, professors, physicians and world leaders dating from Plato to present day. Many of the greatest minds the world has ever known discovered and spoke of the value of humor and laughter, and their words should not be taken lightly. One of the best and fastest ways to learn to navigate our complicated and often confusing lives is to derive knowledge from the experiences of others. Who better to learn from than the wisest of the wise?

Many people hold the view that humor is frivolous, anti-intellectual and not "cool," but they believe this at their own peril and miss out on one of the greatest natural sources of joy in life. Hopefully the contents of this book will change some of those minds and bring greater understanding and appreciation for the value of all that makes us giggle, laugh and guffaw.

To those who avoid comedic opportunities in an effort to preserve a reputation as a serious professional or intellectual, philosopher Ludwig Wittgenstein said, "Never stay up on the barren heights of cleverness, but come down into the green valleys of silliness." Widely regarded as the greatest philosopher of the 20th century, he speaks words of wisdom.

BIBLIOGRAPHY

Bergeson, Henri. 1999. *Laughter: An Essay on the Meaning of the Comic*. Los Angeles: Green Integer.

Billig, Michael. 2005. *Laughter and Ridicule: Towards a Social Critique of Humor.* London: Sage Publications.

Bowen, John. 2006. *Why the French Don't Like Headscarves. Islam, the State, and Public Space.* Princeton: Princeton University Press.

Bressler, Eric R.; Martin, Rod A., and Balshine, Sigal. 2006. *Production and Appreciation of Humor as Sexually Selected Traits.* As cited in *The Journal of Evolution and Human Behavior*, Vol. 27.

Crawford, Mary. 1995. *Talking Differences: On Gender and Language.* London: Sage.

Gilbert, Joanne. 2004. *Performing Marginality: Humor, Gender, and Cultural Critique.* Detroit: Wayne State University Press.

Klein, Allen. 1989. *The Healing Power of Humor.* Los Angeles: Tarcher Press.

Lefcourt, Herbert M. 2000. *Humor: The Psychology of Living Buoyantly.* The Springer Series in Social Clinical Psychology.

Lewis, Paul. 2006. *Cracking Up: American Humor in a Time of Conflict.* Chicago: University of Chicago Press.

Lipman, Steve. 1991. *Laughter in Hell: The Use of Humor During the Holocaust.* Northvale, New Jersey: Jason Aronson Inc.

Martin, Rod A. 2007. *The Psychology of Humor: An Integrative Approach.* Burlington, MA: Elsevier Academic Press.

McLaughlin, Kim. 2008. *Danish cartoonist says has no regrets.* Reuters, March 26, 2008.

Morreall, John. 1987. *The Philosophy of Laughter and Humor.* New York: State University of New York Press.

Mulkay, Michael. 1988. *On Humour: Its Nature and Place in Modern Society.* Oxford: Blackwell Publishing.

Obrdlik, Antonin J. 1942. *Gallows Humor: A Sociological Phenomenon.* As cited in *The American Journal of Sociology, Vol. 47.*

Oring, Elliott. 1983. *The People of the Joke: On the Conceptualization of a Jewish Humor.* Berkeley: University of California Press.

Provine, Robert R. 2000. *Laughter: A Scientific Investigation.* New York: Penguin Books.

Reichsgesetz-blatt I. 1941. Article 1, sections 1 and 3. Cited in *Schmulowitz.*

Restak, Richard. 2006. *The Naked Brain: How the Emerging Neurosociety Is Changing How We Live, Work and Love.* New York: Harmony Books.

Schwartz, Jeffrey M. and Begley, Sharon. 2003. *The Mind and the Brain: Neuroplasticity and the Power of Mental Force.* New York: HarperCollins.

Shaw, B.D. 1939. *Is Hitler Dead? And the Best Anti-Nazi Humor.* New York: Alcaeus House.

Slackman, Michael. 2006. *Iran exhibits anti-Jewish arts as reply to Danish cartoons.* New York Times, August 25, 2006.

Strauch, Barbara. 2010. *The Secret Life of the Grown-Up Brain: The Surprising Talents of the Middle-Aged Mind.* New York: Viking.

Wickberg, Daniel. 1998. *The Senses of Humor: Self and Laughter in Modern America.* Ithaca: Cornell University Press.

NICHOLE FORCE, M.A.

Life in itself is neither good nor evil.
It is the place of good and evil,
according to what you make it.

~Montaigne

3179674R00081

Printed in Great Britain
by Amazon.co.uk, Ltd.,
Marston Gate.